D0387106

AN
AMERICAN
PRINCESS

AN AMERICAN PRINCESS

The Many Lives of Allene Tew

Annejet
van der Zijl

Translated by Michele Hutchison

amazoncrossing ⊚

Text copyright © 2015 by Annejet van der Zijl

Translation copyright © 2018 by Michele Hutchison

All rights reserved.

No part of this book may be reproduced, or stored in a retrieval system, or transmitted in any form or by any means, electronic, mechanical, photocopying, recording, or otherwise, without express written permission of the publisher.

Previously published as *De Amerikaanse prinses* by Querido in the Netherlands in 2015. Translated from Dutch by Michele Hutchison. First published in English by AmazonCrossing in 2018.

Published by AmazonCrossing, Seattle

www.apub.com

Amazon, the Amazon logo, and AmazonCrossing are trademarks of Amazon.com, Inc., or its affiliates.

ISBN-13: 9781503951839 (hardcover)
ISBN-10: 1503951839 (hardcover)

ISBN-13: 9781542049740 (paperback)
ISBN-10: 1542049741 (paperback)

Cover design by PEPE *nymi*

Printed in the United States of America
First edition

The Marriages of Allene Tew

Charles Tew (1849–1925) x 1871 Jennette Smith (1840–1923)

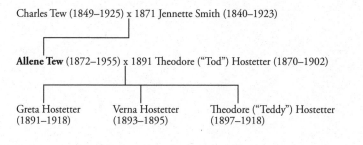

Allene Tew (1872–1955) x 1891 Theodore ("Tod") Hostetter (1870–1902)

Greta Hostetter
(1891–1918)

Verna Hostetter
(1893–1895)

Theodore ("Teddy") Hostetter
(1897–1918)

x 1904 **Morton Nichols** (1870–1932)

x 1912 **Anson Burchard** (1865–1927)

x 1929 **Henry Reuss** (Prince Heinrich xxxiii Reuss, 1879–1942)
Marlisa (Princess Marie Luise Reuss, 1915–1985)
Heiner (Prince Heinrich ii Reuss, 1916–1993)

x 1936 **Paul Kotzebue** (Pavel Pavlovitch Kotzebue, 1884–1966)

AN
AMERICAN
PRINCESS

PROLOGUE

The Blue Room I

Winter 1954–1955

Picture this: an old woman and the sea.

The woman was old and not even a shadow of the beauty she had once been. The sea was cold and wild and looked nothing like the blue idyll of the summer. And the house she was staying in had been built as a holiday home; it was an entirely unsuitable place to spend the winter, let alone to convalesce—or to die.

Old age and illness are destroyers of individuality. Just as babies look alike, so do people at the end of their lives. Those who stay in their birthplace may escape this fate somewhat if they still have people around them who know what they used to look like when they were in their prime. But this woman hadn't stayed where she was born. On the contrary, she had allowed herself to be chased away, across the world—by fate, by her restlessness, or by a combination of the two. And now she had washed up in a ramshackle, drafty sea palace on the other side of the world, and there was nobody left who could pay testament to her youth or her beauty, her previous lives and loves, her lost ones, or the dramatic Technicolor movie of her life.

Day and night the waves crashed onto the rocks beneath the house. And up there in the Blue Room, illness raged, as impetuous and stubborn as the waves. Her life slowly shrank until it was only a matter of months, weeks, days; the next minute, the next breath. As long as she kept breathing, she was still alive. As long as she lay awake at night and heard the sea, she was still there.

In fact, her true self existed only in the pile of yellowing photographs next to her bed, and in memories that danced among the rushing and ebbing waves of sea and pain and flared in the flames of the log fire that had been kept burning day and night these past months. For if you no longer have a future, what else is there left but dreams of the past?

1

Uncle George's Cabin

Green—that was the color of the landscape of Allene's youth. From the delicate green in the springtime, when young leaves spread themselves across the trees like net curtains, to the dark, heavy green of late summer foliage. From the bright green of the beeches to the grayish blue green of the firs and, in between, the very different shades of chestnuts, maples, birches, and cherry and walnut trees—the totality like a natural arboretum draped across the hills around Lake Chautauqua. Until the fall, when those trees burst into a fiesta of reds, oranges, and yellows before shriveling up in the freezing temperatures that blew down from Canada and the dark winter storms that blasted across the large watery expanses of Lake Erie.

Then only the tops of the trees stuck out above a thick, thick layer of snow. The lake ossified into a silent black mirror, and the hills receded into a black-and-white landscape, with just the fierce red of a streaking fox to remind people that color still existed. They kept the fires burning day and night in the houses, which were themselves huddled under thick blankets of snow, enabling the inhabitants to survive the harsh winters of North America.

With those fires begins the story of Allene Tew and her family in Jamestown, New York. And, almost at the same time, the story of the place itself begins, for the Tews were among the first young adventurers who dared build their futures on the then still-impenetrable and dangerous wilderness around the lake.

Even before the Tews, though, the origins of Jamestown could be found in four covered wagons and one family. In 1806, the Prendergasts set off from Rensselaer County, in New York State's Hudson Valley. The travelers—twenty-nine men, women, and children—headed from this region just east of New York City in search of new opportunities and, most important, fertile and still-unclaimed land. In fact, the Prendergasts were planning to travel to the large expanses of Tennessee, where land was being granted to anyone dogged enough to survive there.

While still in New York, the travelers stopped beside a beautifully situated elongated lake in Chautauqua County. There they were approached by an agent from Holland Land Company, a Dutch banking conglomerate that had acquired more than three million acres a few years previously and was now trying to palm chunks of it off onto pioneers.

The agent told them to look around: "This is the paradise of the New World."

And indeed, the Creator had done his very best in this part of the world. The hills around the lake were green and fertile, without the marshes or bald mountain massifs that often formed impediments in other regions. The summers were warm and wet, perfect for agriculture. Eighteen-mile-long Lake Chautauqua was brimming with fish, mainly pike and perch. And the uncultivated wilderness around it was swarming with animals that were used for fur and food: beavers, bears, otters, foxes, wolves, and deer, even panthers and other wild cats. The area was also rich in birdlife, particularly in the fall, when the view of the lake was almost blotted out by the numerous flapping flocks of ducks, cranes, herons, and swans.

And so the family from Rensselaer County changed their plans. Wagons were anchored, paperwork signed. In total, the Prendergasts bought 3,337 acres on the north side of Lake Chautauqua, upon which they would build their new life.

It was their youngest son, James Prendergast, who, a few years later, when looking for a group of runaway horses, discovered a flat piece of land near the rapids of the Chadakoin River, approximately three miles south of the lake. At eighteen he hadn't yet come of age, but he had the entrepreneurial spirit of the rest of his family, and he asked his older brother to buy a thousand acres for him at two dollars each. In the summer of 1811, James, with the help of a servant, built a water-powered sawmill with an accompanying cabin, which he moved into with his young wife, Nancy. The loggers working for them built their own even more primitive cabins nearby.

And so—it was that simple in the America of those years— Jamestown was born.

***

It wasn't easy at the start. Life in the wilderness was hard and dangerous, not only because of the bears and other wild animals but also because of the descendants of the Iroquois and Seneca tribes. The area had been their home until French colonists drove them off in the eighteenth century, but the hostility between the settlers and the area's Indian tribes continued.

The winters were long and lonely and brought with them new dangers—twice, the entire encampment, including the mill, burned to the ground. But the pioneers were young and determined, and they rebuilt their tiny village on the Chadakoin River from scratch each time. Two of James's brothers organized a makeshift and irregularly stocked grocer's shop; a veteran of the War of Independence built a pottery-*cum*-tavern; a carpenter from Vermont improvised a carpentry workshop; and shortly after that, the Tew brothers arrived. They cleared a plot of land and built a blacksmith's forge on it.

George and William Tew were also from Rensselaer County. They'd heard news of the promising little settlement deep in the woods through letters the Prendergasts had sent back to their hometown. George was twenty-one and a blacksmith's apprentice by profession. His brother William, who was four years younger, had been trained as a cobbler but had also learned useful skills like spinning, sewing, and furniture making.

While the Tew brothers built cabins, loggers tamed the forest, yard by yard, tree by tree. Every day, the sounds of chopping and sawing rang out, occasionally interrupted by shouting, creaking, or the last sigh of yet another forest giant being brought down. After the trees had been stripped of their branches and bark, they were floated down the river to the mill and sawed into beams and planks. Next the wood was transported by canoes or keelboats to the big cities by the river to the south, along with other merchandise including furs, salted fish, and maple syrup.

For the return journey, the boats were laden with everything the forest dwellers needed and couldn't produce themselves, such as nails, tools, ham, sugar, salt, and dried fruit. Tobacco and plenty of bottles of Monongahela rye, the famous strong whiskey made in Pittsburgh, were also aboard. As were potential new inhabitants, spurred on by the stories of the Jamestowners.

By now, James Prendergast had divided his land into plots of 50 by 120 feet, which he sold to newcomers for fifty dollars apiece. A primitive bridge was built across the Chadakoin River, and the dirt road at a right angle to the river was given the obvious name of Main Street. Equally prosaically, the wagon tracks to the left and right of Main Street were called First Street, Second Street, and so on.

In the early days, James was judge, postmaster, and unofficial mayor, but when the population of his cabin village surpassed four hundred in 1827, the inhabitants organized the first elections for a village council. Blacksmith George Tew, one of the few residents who had mastered the art of reading and writing, was elected village clerk. His first job was to set down on paper the rights and duties of his fellow villagers. Brother William was appointed second man in the fire brigade, the first collective activity the brand-new council took upon itself.

***

In the years that followed, the settlement grew like wildfire. The Industrial Revolution spread to the new continent and had a positive effect on regions like this, where trees ensured unlimited supplies of fuel and the many rivers and streams formed a natural transport network. The arrival of the steamboat made canoes and keelboats superfluous and ensured regular connections with the outside world, something that increased the appeal of this forest village to those in search of new opportunities.

In the cleared areas against the hillsides, farmers now settled— primarily Scandinavians, predisposed to handling the isolation, the primitive living conditions, and the long winters in this still-desolate land. They introduced stock breeding, orchards, beehives, tobacco plants, and the art of woodworking. After a while, real furniture factories rose up on the flat ground down by the river, which for some reason became known as Brooklyn Square and developed into Jamestown's commercial heart.

In the meantime, George Tew enjoyed his position as village clerk so much that he gave up his labors in the hot, sooty blacksmith's shop and became an apprentice to the only lawyer for miles around. After a few years as the lawyer's partner, he was elected county clerk, one of the most important administrative roles in the region, in 1834. This meant that he and his wife and children could move to the town of Mayville, at the northern tip of Lake Chautauqua, where government officials lived.

The blacksmith's shop on the corner of Main and Third Streets was left in the calloused hands of his brother William, who'd also started a family by this time. He was hardly lonely, however, as he had his wife and children, and his father and five sisters had all moved from Rensselaer County to Jamestown. Business was booming—so much that William could move to a brick house that also served as a store and workshop on the corner of Main and Second Streets, close to Brooklyn Square. He took on one of his brothers-in-law as a partner, hired a servant for the heavy work, and renamed the blacksmith's shop the upscale-sounding W. H. Tew's Copper, Tin and Sheet Iron Factory and Stove Store. A German maid was hired to help his wife with the family's six children.

Later, the man who would become Allene's grandfather would be praised in an almanac as being of "high character." According to his biographer, William Tew was a loyal family man, an ardent Republican, and a dedicated member of the Presbyterian Church. Aside from this, he was also the founder of Jamestown's first temperance society. A less well-known role of William's was the one he played in the Underground Railroad, a civilian network that smuggled slaves who had escaped from plantations in the South up to Canada.

One of the few members of the middle class to do so, William advertised openly in the *Liberty Press*, the antislavery movement's newspaper, which, since the publication of *Uncle Tom's Cabin* in 1852, had garnered a lot of support among the North American bourgeoisie. This type of activity was not completely free of danger: there were fines of $1,000 and prison sentences for anyone who helped the escapees, and slave owners would come to Jamestown to locate and demand return of their runaway slaves, if necessary. But the former cobbler's apprentice was by now an established, widely esteemed citizen, which meant he could allow himself the luxury of having principles.

***

William's brother George's star was rising to even greater heights. He had quickly moved beyond provincial government and, as director of the Bank of Silver Creek, was now one of the most influential movers and shakers of Chautauqua County. Members of the business community were lobbying hard to have their region included in the new railway network, which in those years was spreading across the map of North America like the web of a drunken spider.

They succeeded. On August 25, 1860, the people of Jamestown witnessed a spectacle they'd remember for the rest of their lives. In the words of a wildly enthusiastic reporter for the *Jamestown Journal*: "The first iron horse that ever deigned to call in on our town drove majestically across the bridge on Main Street."

In fact, only a small train crawled into the still-very-provisional station in Jamestown, but it was still a great wonder. There was now a direct connection to cities like New York, Chicago, and Pittsburgh via the Atlantic and Great Western Railroad. Within a single lifetime, a primitive collection of cabins that was once only reachable by horse or canoe had grown into a city of the world.

The railway line gave wings to the woodworking industry, and Jamestown furniture soon became a household name across the entire United States. The textile industry flourished, too. As if the gods hadn't looked down kindly enough upon the inhabitants, they provided another lucrative and entirely free export product in the form of large ice blocks, which could be hacked out of the frozen lake in the winter and transported by train to gigantic ice houses in the big cities. In this way, the lake played an indirect role in the revolution the introduction of cooled produce created in kitchens, as well as the great success America had on the global food market.

The Civil War broke out in April 1861, and it seemed that this development might hamper Jamestown's success. Four years later, on April 9,

1865, the North was victorious. Slavery was abolished, and the Southern states lost a great deal of their economic and political clout. The ink on the capitulation agreement was barely dry before the economy in the North was booming as never before. The banking sector that had financed military efforts had done excellent business during the war, and the ever-entrepreneurial George Tew, together with his five adult sons, had set up his own bank. The Second National Bank of Jamestown made the onetime blacksmith's helper one of Jamestown's richest men in his old age. He became even more influential when all of his sons managed to marry girls from the region's most prominent families, like the Prendergasts.

Just as successful in work and marriage was Harvey, William Tew's oldest son. After working for his father in the family business for seventeen years, in 1870 Harvey established a rubber factory with his brother-in-law Benjamin F. Goodrich. The story goes that the pair came up with the idea after large fires swept through Jamestown, which still consisted mainly of wooden buildings, sometimes wiping out entire neighborhoods. In winter, the fire brigade was repeatedly rendered powerless when the water froze in its leather hoses. The discovery that water stayed liquid in rubber hoses made the fortunes of Harvey and his brother-in-law and formed the basis of a company that would grow into one of the world's largest tire producers.

***

But there was one Tew who hadn't effortlessly followed in the first generation's successful footsteps, and that was the man who would become Allene's father: Charles, William's youngest son. He was born in 1849, the last male descendant in the second generation, and it was as though the available supply of energy and ambition had simply run out. While his brother and cousins had long been working in their fathers' businesses by the time they reached the age of fifteen, Charles was still at school. And while every one of his cousins made socially beneficial matches, in 1871 Charles married Jennette Smith, the nine-years-older daughter of a local liveryman who also worked as a coachman and postman. Not only was Charles's father-in-law from a significantly lower class than the Tew family, he was also a Southerner, from Tennessee.

The young couple must have been aware of their status as the less successful branch of the family. After the wedding, Charles and Jennette settled down in the sparsely populated countryside of Wisconsin, where there was still free land to be had for aspiring farmers. There, in the tiny village of Janesville in Rock County, Allene was born on July 7, 1872. Hers was an unusual name, probably a variant of the Irish *Eileen*, and one that might have sounded more chic to Charles and Jennette.

Charles wasn't cut out to be a pioneer, it transpired, and soon the young couple returned to Jamestown and moved into Jennette's father's livery stable on West Third Avenue. Charles's father, William, had given up his business on Main Street to take over his late brother George's role as president of the family bank. He had passed the stove and hardware store to his daughter, who had married his former helper. Charles was found an unchallenging job as assistant cashier in the bank.

And thus Allene spent the first years of her life in the commotion and equine stench of a livery in the center of Jamestown, unlike her many cousins who lived in expensive mansions on the leafy outskirts of the town. Only later, when her grandfather William withdrew from the bank, moved to a detached house on Pine Street, and had his youngest son and his wife and child come and live next to him, did she get a more distinguished place of residence.

It was clear that Allene would remain an only child—an unusual phenomenon in a prolific clan like the Tews. Also clear was that her father would never make it beyond cashier. He would be the only second-generation Tew male in Jamestown never to be lauded in the almanacs in which the era's most prominent citizens of the region were portrayed.

***

On July 4, 1876, Americans celebrated one hundred years of independence. And celebrate they did, with a passion; seldom had a country
been able to offer its inhabitants as many opportunities as the United
States could at that moment. It was a massive, still largely virgin country
full of valuable resources like wood, rivers, and ore. New technologies
and inventions were the order of the day, and there was an almost
unequaled mentality of ambition and daring. Everything seemed to be
conspiring not only to give Americans the "right to life, liberty and the
pursuit of happiness," as set down in the Declaration of Independence,
but also to make that happiness genuinely possible.

The continent was bursting at the seams with revelry, and Jamestown
proved itself up to the task. "We will celebrate!" the local newspaper
had announced, months in advance. The city was dolled up like a factory girl on her wedding day, and on the great day itself, an immense
parade of bands, the fire brigade, and sports associations passed through
triumphal archways decorated with flowers. There were concerts, dance
parties, and picnics everywhere, and in the evening a large fireworks
display over Lake Chautauqua propelled the country into the next century. "How we celebrated," the *Jamestown Journal* sighed the next day.
"Twenty thousand people come to the front—and go home happy!"

In subsequent years, new inventions like the combustion engine
and developments like the large-scale application of steel heralded
the arrival of a second Industrial Revolution, and prosperity in North
America became unstoppable. The United States' share of worldwide
industrial output grew to 30 percent, almost as much as that of its former motherland, England, which had considered itself the undisputed
leader of the world's economy up to that point.

The Americans, who had been dependent on Europe for many
of their resources before the Civil War, now began to export prod-
ucts back to the Old World at competitive prices. Entrepreneurs, still
unhindered by limiting factors like income tax or trade regulations,

made unprecedented fortunes in a matter of years. Origin had become unimportant—only individual ambition, cleverness, and daring mattered. The number of millionaires grew, in a few decades, from twenty to forty thousand. The American population tripled between 1865 and 1900 but became, as a whole, a whopping thirteen times richer.

Everything seemed possible in the Gilded Age, as Mark Twain called this period of national expansion and unbridled optimism. Paupers came in rags on boats from Europe and worked themselves up to being millionaires. The attraction of this country of unlimited opportunities had never been greater for fortune hunters than it was now. During the first half of the nineteenth century, around two and a half million immigrants risked the ocean crossing; during the second half, the stream swelled to a dazzling eleven million.

So perhaps Allene's father wasn't a success story like the rest of her family, and perhaps her rich cousins and classmates at the Jamestown Union School considered that a reason to treat her with a certain pity, but young as she was, she held her head high. And for good reason, in the scarce childhood photographs of her that are known, it is apparent that Allene Tew inherited one thing that couldn't be obtained with money: beauty. She grew up with something better than wealth, a dream—the American dream, in which you could become whatever you wanted, wherever you came from. In which, as her great-uncle George and her grandfather had proved, you could start out in a primitive cabin in the middle of the hostile wilderness and end up in a marble bank building in a booming city, a city that you had wrested from the woods with your bare hands.

2

The Glittering Paradise

Years later, when she was an old woman and no longer needed or was able to worry about her own children, Allene wrote of the possessive urge parents often felt and how important it was not to succumb to it:

> Everyone has the right to live her own life, NO parent can destroy the youth and joy of their child. They use all kinds of excuses to try and cover their selfishness but if the daughter or son do take the bit in their teeth and LIVE the mother always gets on allright.

"Everyone has the right to live her own life . . ." And it sounds as though Allene had personal experience testing that. And so she had. If there was ever a girl in Jamestown who gave her parents reason to worry, it was Allene.

Charles and Jennette Tew may have been able to keep their beautiful, impetuous daughter in check if Jamestown had remained the rugged yet uninspiring pioneer community it had been during their youth. That this didn't happen was, ironically enough, the fault of Methodists and other religious groups who, halfway through the 1870s, discovered in Chautauqua the earthly paradise of their dreams.

On the northern side of the still lovely and unspoiled Lake Chautauqua, the Methodists built the Chautauqua Institution, a kind of permanent summer colony created to promote all sorts of edifying subjects, such as art, science, religion, patriotism, and education. The institution soon attracted important visitors, such as the inventor Thomas Edison, the writer Rudyard Kipling, and, in 1880, even President James Garfield. When he left, Garfield devoted a lyrical speech to the place: "It has been the struggle of the world to get more leisure, but it was left for Chautauqua to show how to use it."

Rich inhabitants of big cities like Cleveland, Chicago, and Pittsburgh didn't need to be told twice. They'd show the world how people should put their free time to good use. From the early 1880s, the banks of Lake Chautauqua were gradually clad in wood—in hotels and summerhouses built in neo-Gothic style, each more expensive and luxurious than the next, intended for "the Wealth and Fashion from leading American cities." And along with flirting men in their carefree straw boater hats and women in their elegant summer outfits, Glamour and her little sister Frivolity also arrived in Chautauqua.

The city dwellers came by train, followed by streams of servants and stacks of travel trunks. On the Jamestown docks, they transferred to the white steamboats, elegantly decorated with filigree, of the Great White Fleet that sailed across the lake from six o'clock in the morning until midnight without interruption. In the evening, the boats, romantically lit by oil lamps, were used for moonlight cruises and transportation to and from the many dance parties, concerts, theater shows, vaudevilles, straw rides, dinners, and other forms of entertainment organized for the summer guests.

And so Allene grew up in a world with two faces. In early May, when nature burst out from under the last remains of the snow, the shutters of lakeside fairy-tale palaces would open and everything would be readied for the short, hot, festive summer season. At the end of August, when the trees began to change color, the party would end as abruptly as it had begun. The shutters would be closed; the lake would again become the quiet domain of flocks of migratory birds and a few solitary fishermen. And Jamestown would return to its mundane, wintery self: an essentially sober, God-fearing town, moderate in everything except its ambitions.

***

The inhabitants of Jamestown looked on the annual summer invasion with mixed feelings. It was true that holidaymakers brought money and prosperity, and the townspeople were businesslike enough to take advantage of this down to the last cent. But the summer visitors also introduced to Chautauqua all the ailments of modern city life that the townspeople, as true Victorians, were so very afraid of: godlessness, gambling, alcohol, promiscuity, and—heaven forbid—fallen women and unwanted pregnancies. The rich young bachelors who treated the lake as their favorite playground during those years were particularly regarded with suspicion. They gambled and they drank; they swam in money and seemed to have little else to do than turn the heads of as many local girls as possible.

Girls such as Allene Tew, for example. Perhaps because it was unclear which class she belonged to, always floating from the livery stable of her mother's family on the one side to the Tews' bank building on the other. Perhaps, too, because she was the only child of rather passive parents and lacked the tight harness of a larger family. In any case, she was different, freer than her female cousins and peers and considerably less inclined to act like a lady as it was then defined.

Her grandfather Andrew Smith, the coachman, had instilled in Allene a great love of horses. She could ride like a boy—and often better than one. And she was clever; she had, a friend would later attest, "a quick wit and a daring that became her." Quick wit and daring weren't the only things that suited her. With her dark blond hair, pale blue eyes, and elegant figure, she was unmistakably a young woman every man would look at—"a blue-eyed blonde with defiantly arched eyebrows," as she once was described.

Allene's gaze indeed contrasted with the humility and modesty preached as typical feminine virtues during that period. Perhaps, those eyes said, her parents weren't endowed with the unbridled dynamism of the Tews, but she was. She longed for pleasure, for adventure, and particularly for a world that was larger than the essentially small-town Jamestown.

In short, Allene Tew had everything anyone might need to get into trouble. And that is what she did.

***

Theodore "Tod" Hostetter was the nightmare incarnate of every father in Jamestown. "Charming . . . rakish . . . a gay Lothario, as reckless as he was handsome" was how a journalist friend of his characterized him. He could amply afford his arrogance because even though this heir from Pittsburgh was scarcely twenty years old the first time he met Allene, he had already received such an improbably large fortune that all he had to do for the rest of his life was spend it as creatively as possible.

Tod had his father, David Hostetter, to thank for the excess of dollars. David's life story contained precisely the magical mix of elements that convinced immigrants all over the world to jump on boats to America. Raised as the son of a village doctor in a sparsely populated, poor farming region in Pennsylvania, David had tried to make his fortune as a young man during the gold rush in California. When gold turned out to be more difficult to find than first thought, he opened a grocery store, which soon burned down. After that, he returned home, his tail between his legs, with no other future before him than the heavy, physically exhausting existence of a railway laborer.

But David never abandoned his dream of becoming rich, and when he was thirty-four, he came up with the idea of commercially exploiting his father's home-brewed herbal elixir. Dr. J. Hostetter's Celebrated Stomach Bitters proved a resounding success right from its introduction in 1854. It was sold as a remedy for ailments as diverse as stomachaches, bowel complaints, nervousness, and depression, and the Union Army even purchased it on a large scale as a cure for diarrhea during the Civil War.

Years later, when its secret recipe was finally analyzed, it would become clear why it made every patient feel significantly better. In addition to containing some herbs and water, the potion turned out to be loaded with alcohol—estimates vary from 32 to a whopping 47 percent. At a time when antialcohol campaigners such as Allene's grandfather William were managing to banish liquor from public life, the herbal remedy became an attractive alternative.

For David Hostetter, the elixir was a gold mine. The ingredients cost next to nothing, and because he had patented the concoction as a medicine, he didn't need to pay any tax on the profits. In the early 1860s, he was selling more than 450,000 bottles of herbal elixir a year. He kept away suspicious inspectors and teetotalers by publicly making himself known as a devout supporter of prohibition, and he kept his competitors at an appropriate distance with incentives such as a free almanac he produced and made available every December at American grocery stores.

Aside from weather forecasts, agricultural tips, astrological information, and cartoons, *Hostetter's United States Almanac for the Use of Merchants, Mechanics, Farmers, Planters and all Families* was full of anecdotes about the miraculous healing powers of Hostetter's Bitters. During this period, it was the only book in many American households, aside from the Bible. "They can talk about Shakespeare, but in my opinion old Hostetter . . . had more influence on the national life than any of 'em," an influential columnist wrote.

By the early 1870s, David was selling more than a million bottles a year. He invested the gigantic profits he made in all kinds of rising industries in and around Pittsburgh, such as railways, mining, the banking sector, and oil extraction, something for which his failed adventures in the Wild West came in handy. The former railway laborer now moved as an equal alongside such famous Gilded Age millionaires as Cornelius Vanderbilt, John D. Rockefeller, and Andrew Carnegie. He was on the boards of various prestigious companies like the Pittsburgh and Lake Erie Railroad, the Fort Pitt National Bank, the Pittsburgh Natural Gas Company, and the South Pennsylvania Railroad.

But all those herbal elixirs and all the prestige and money in the world couldn't protect David Hostetter from his own mortality. In 1888, he died at age sixty-nine in a Park Avenue hotel from complications following a kidney operation. He left his widow and three children a fortune of $18 million. Aside from this, all four of them received from the company an annual dividend of $810,000 each—this in a period when the average hourly wage of an American worker was exactly twenty-two cents.

***

In Jamestown, *Hostetter's Almanac* had long been in every household. And there were frequent articles with provocative headlines in the *Jamestown Journal* that, upon closer examination, turned out to be veiled advertisements for the eponymous herbal elixir. It could hardly have escaped Allene's notice that the handsome dark-haired young man she met at a dance in the summer of 1890, and who courted her with his mercurial charm, was heir to one of the largest fortunes in Pittsburgh.

The chance that this Tod Hostetter would reveal himself to be a serious marriage candidate was negligible. America was the land of unprecedented opportunity, but this didn't mean class consciousness didn't exist. On the contrary, now especially, as the country was flooded with millionaires, the existing elite withdrew into a social fortress in which lineage and name were of utter importance. Caroline Astor, the uncrowned queen of New York society, refused to host in her salon even the Vanderbilts, at the time the richest family in the United States—only because their forefather, Cornelius, had begun his career as a ferry boy and his descendants behaved in a fashion too unorthodox in her eyes for them to be classified as ladies and gentlemen.

"Mrs. Astor," as all of America knew her, was descended from the Knickerbockers, the British and Dutch pioneers who had set the tone of American society since colonial times. She considered it her personal mission to prove that she and her countrymen were more than the tobacco-chewing illiterate bumpkins the world took them for. After Georges Clemenceau—who would eventually become French prime minister—announced in 1889 that America had gone from barbarism to hedonism "without achieving any civilization between the two," Mrs. Astor drew up a list of the four hundred people who in her view counted as a kind of American aristocracy. The chosen ones could boast of not only an impeccable way of life but also fortunes that could be traced back at least three generations.

As happens when anything can be bought except social status, trying to prove themselves in Mrs. Astor's eyes became a true mania among the wives of the nouveaux riches. Handbooks like *The Laws of Etiquette, or Short Rules and Reflections for Conduct in Society* were studied closely, and any decent American town had its own social register, or blue book—a directory of families who were worthy of being received in polite society. Even Tod's mother had acted in this race to respectability. Although her husband's money was certainly new and smelled just a little too strongly of alcohol to be respectable, she still managed to have her two oldest children marry scions of old, prominent Pittsburgh families.

The last thing Rosetta Hostetter needed was a liaison between her son and a girl without social status, means, or useful connections and from a region that, compared to metropolitan Pittsburgh, counted as the sticks. For this reason, the lovers kept their budding summer romance on Lake Chautauqua strictly secret at first. It remained so—even in the late summer, when the season's visitors had left Chautauqua and Tod was expected to resume his medical studies. And even after Allene, in the heart of the cold winter of 1891, discovered that the clandestine meetings with her Pittsburgh admirer had not been without consequence. She was pregnant.

***

It was the end of the nineteenth century, and Victorian standards of propriety were followed to the letter. Men and women lived in completely separate worlds, and the bourgeoisie was so prudish that piano, chair, and table legs were covered and any thoughts that drifted toward sexuality were to be fended off. And if there was one sin that a respectable, unmarried girl in this age could not commit, it was to become pregnant.

Many a young woman in Allene's position ended her life to spare herself and her family a scandal. Young men such as Tod, in turn, usually withdrew from girlfriends who had been so stupid and wanton as to let this happen. They'd have their father, an older brother, or the family lawyer buy off their former lover and then settle down in the safety of their family fortune, their respectable future, and the unblemished wife who went with it.

But Allene hadn't been stupid. Her Tod might have been a gay libertine, but he was also kindhearted and genuinely crazy about her. On top of this, as a cherished and spoiled youngest child, he was accustomed to his family members ultimately letting him get away with things, however despairing they were of his antics at first. And so he and Allene resorted to the only possibility open to lovers wanting to stay together against their parents' wishes: an elopement. They ran away, all the way to New York City, where, on May 14, 1891, they were secretly married in the Church of the Heavenly Rest on the corner of Fifth Avenue and Forty-Fifth Street.

In a final attempt to save the honor of the daughter who had so suddenly disappeared from town, Charles and Jennette Tew announced the news to the world in the *Jamestown Evening Journal*. The birth of the baby who had triggered this would be advertised in the same place exactly ten months later—conveniently failing to mention the fact that the infant was already five months old.

Allene's past in Jamestown was now over, but her future in Pittsburgh was just beginning. Tod's family, suddenly confronted with a highly unwelcome, undesired, and poorly timed marriage, didn't think for a minute of advertising this blot on the family crest in the various Pittsburgh chronicles that reported every last move made by a blue-book family.

When, days after the marriage, the couple took the train from New York to Pittsburgh, Allene could see the black cloud hanging above her new home from a long way off. There was an actual cloud, originating from the thousands of chimneys that incessantly poured out smoke and soot. This was "Smoky Town," after all. But there was also an invisible cloud: her rejection by her new family, who considered the baby in her belly a scandal and her a sophisticated gold digger who had managed to ensnare their naive youngest son.

***

As green and fresh as had been the world in which Allene grew up, so gray and airless was the place where she arrived as the young Mrs. Hostetter. During the Industrial Revolution, Pittsburgh had—thanks to its strategic placement on the Allegheny, the Monongahela, and the

Ohio Rivers and the rich coal deposits in the soil—become one of the richest cities in North America. In those years, the city housed more millionaires than even New York. But it was also one of the dirtiest and certainly one of the most dreary places on the continent.

The so-called Golden Triangle, the plain between the three rivers where the city of Pittsburgh had been founded, was in fact a gigantic, heavily polluted industrial zone. Among the blast furnaces that burned day and night, the glass and leather factories, and the warehouses for petroleum, gas, and oil were slums and tenements. Here lived all those who had ended up on the wrong side of the American dream in circumstances that rendered downtown Pittsburgh what one inhabitant would express as "hell with the lid taken off."

Of course the robber barons, as the industrialists and factory owners were known because of their unscrupulous practices, did not insult their noses or spoil their views with the exploited and disenfranchised workers of the proletariat. They built their mansions in still-unpolluted small towns and villages in the hills around the city, like Allegheny City, on the north bank of the river of the same name. Predominantly since the Civil War, this former farming village had developed into a real millionaires' mecca, complete with attractive parks, music pavilions, and its own zoo.

There, on a Western Avenue freshly laid especially for rich inhabitants, Tod's father had built a manor house in 1868. The house itself, with its heavy wooden wainscoting and leadlight windows, looked rather old-fashioned by now. But it still counted as one of the most attractive in the area, if only because it was on a double plot, unlike neighboring houses. Tod had been born and raised there, and perhaps for this reason, his father had left it to him in his will.

Up to the moment when his young bride moved to Allegheny, Tod had shared his parental home with his mother and his eleven-years-older brother, David Jr., often called Herbert. Tod's only sister lived with her husband and children on the opposite side of Western Avenue, where, with good foresight, their father had bought a couple of extra plots of land in 1868. These came in handy now, since Tod's mother was less than keen to share the house she had ruled over for more than thirty years with the daughter-in-law she'd had forced upon her so against her wishes. She packed her bags and moved into the house next door to her daughter's.

The serious and responsible Herbert, who had taken on the daily running of the family business after his father's death, wasn't looking forward to Allene's arrival, either. He and his wife moved near to his parents-in-law on "Millionaires' Row," an even richer neighborhood to the east of Pittsburgh. Later he would use the example of his brother's marriage as a deterrent when bringing up his own children:

> A great deal of the trouble in the world comes from too early or willful romances. Therefore, if one kept a boy always with boys and away from the girls, and vice versa, "love's disturbing element" could not enter into their lives.

***

And so love's disturbing element began her new life in Pittsburgh in the form of the now visibly pregnant Allene. She and Tod shared the large house at 171 Western Avenue with eight members of staff, most of whom had been in service to Rosetta, Tod's mother, for years. American servants were famous for being considerably ruder than their European colleagues. That, coupled with the fact that the staff must have been aware of the details surrounding Allene's marriage to their young master *and* the fact that their very young new mistress wasn't exactly from the upper crust, must have made her role as head of housekeeping even harder.

Allene's reception into her husband's family might have been icy and the atmosphere in the dark lump of stone on Western Avenue not much warmer, but it did get hot in the months that followed. The summers in the south of Pennsylvania were known for stuffy heat that often persisted for weeks, and the more temperatures rose, the more the stench and smoke from the hellhole that was downtown Pittsburgh blew toward their green town in the hills. Houses and gardens were covered in a thin layer of soot, which, however assiduously the servants washed and scrubbed, could never be entirely cleaned away.

This was why the rich of Allegheny would prepare at the end of June for their annual exodus to cooler and fresher parts. The Hostetters usually departed for their holiday home in Narragansett Pier, a seaside resort on a Rhode Island bay. Shore Acres, which Tod's father had built, was on Ocean Drive and had cool sea breezes galore and a panoramic view of the Atlantic Ocean. The house had sixteen rooms, but the family did not want Tod and his now very pregnant wife to stay there: Narragansett Pier was close to Newport, New York society's regular summer colony where Mrs. Astor held her famous summer ball in her country house, Beechwood. An invitation to this indicated the pinnacle of success, since it came with automatic admission to the very highest social echelons of the country.

And so reputations in and around Newport had to be tended with particular care. Tod must have understood that his family absolutely could not permit any suggestion of having accepted his wife as one of their own, not after the damaging spring they'd had to endure.

***

Allene might have been still young and, in the beginning, still in awe of what a journalist friend of hers later described as "the glittering paradise of the Hostetters, where jewels were for the mere hint and money flowed like a veritable Niagara." But even back then, she wasn't the kind of woman to spend the entire summer closeted away in boiling-hot Pennsylvania. And so on July 5, 1891, a week before the official start of the ten-week summer season, the *New York Times* ran a notice that a "Mrs. Hostetter of Allegheny City" had rented a cottage on a small island facing Narragansett Pier that happened, perhaps by coincidence, to be called Jamestown.

Summer life in "Jimtown," as regular visitors affectionately called the windswept rocky island, was completely different than in prim and ostentatiously wealthy summer colonies like Newport and Narragansett Pier. The cottages, built in the local shingle style, were fairly primitive and furnished with lightweight wicker furniture. Entertainment was equally unpretentious and consisted mainly of simple pleasures like walking, paddling in the sea, picnics, and looking for shells. As one visitor described it:

> All guests were given free use of the resources of the house, rocks and harbor, and were expected to do exactly as they liked. Some sat inside playing the piano, some sat outside playing the guitar or banjo, some sat in rocking chairs, some on the grass . . . Some played tennis or quoits, some rowed, and a fine party of young folks went swimming off the pier, diving or jumping off its rail. And whatever we did, we sang in doing it.

While Allene enjoyed the relaxed atmosphere, Tod spent most of his time "Grand Yachting," a favorite sport of the Gilded Age millionaires. The spacious, deep, and sheltered bay off Rhode Island was exceptionally well suited to their very expensive steam sailing yachts equipped with all the creature comforts. America's wealth had increased spectacularly, and in the summer the bay turned white with sails.

Tod's ship, the *Judy*, was nearly a hundred feet long, had a permanent six-man crew, and had been designed by the famous yacht builder Nathanael Herreshoff. But however elegant the $25,000 ship was, there was no question of Tod being able to moor it in Newport, where the country's most prestigious nautical club, the New York Yacht Club, had its own jetty and clubhouse. The yacht club was as famous for protecting its waterfront from socially undesirable elements as Mrs. Astor was for her ballroom, and there was no way this young and not-all-that-respectable Pittsburgh millionaire would have gotten through the voting process.

This was why Tod followed the example of William K. Vanderbilt, who, after being refused membership to the conservative New York men's clubs, had set up his own Metropolitan Club. On July 14, 1891, Tod founded the Jamestown Yacht Club, together with a number of other yacht owners. He was elected first commodore—which in practice meant he was the person who paid everyone's bills at the end of the day. And since, besides sailing, Tod was also mad about cards and other gambling games, a few weeks later, the sailing club gained a younger sister in the form of the Jamestown Card Club. The card club, according to its founding treaty, was intended to advance "Social Enjoyment among the Members." Or rather, in the spirit of this wealthy young couple, entirely and only the pleasure of its members.

***

Allene had clearly inherited one thing from her pioneering forefathers, and that was the conviction that if there wasn't a road, there must be a detour that would get you where you wanted to go. And if there wasn't a detour, a road had to be built. "If one has the will and persistence, one CAN do things," she wrote later.

She'd shown this mentality when she organized a vacation house the summer she wasn't welcome at her in-laws'. She showed it again when her daughter Greta, born on September 27, 1891, was as stubbornly ignored by her new milieu as she was. In his official capacity as vice president of the Hostetter business, Tod was accepted as a member of one of the leading gentlemen's clubs in Pittsburgh. But his wife and daughter didn't even get a mention in the *Pittsburgh and Allegheny Blue Book* directory, in which his mother had featured for years as the embodiment of Victorian feminine virtues:

> In her tastes Mrs. Hostetter is thoroughly domestic; famous as a housekeeper, the best sort of wife, and as a mother simply adorable. Mrs. Hostetter dresses in excellent taste, in a style entirely suitable for her years.

This meant total social isolation for Allene. She was not invited anywhere, she couldn't leave her visiting card anywhere, and no one came to visit her. It was as though she and Greta simply did not exist.

Again a detour was necessary, and again Allene found one. It was in the impressive form of the Daughters of the American Revolution, one of the most exclusive of the women's clubs shooting out of the ground like mushrooms at the time. In most cases, these clubs functioned as covert vehicles to higher social positions. The DAR had been set up in 1890 with the official goal to keep alive the memory of America's ancestors and advance education in remote areas. Membership was restricted to the descendants of people who had fought in the War of Independence.

In December 1892, Allene signed up for the Pittsburgh branch of the DAR. She filled in her lineage on the application with great precision. Her bloodline went back to a British immigrant from Northamptonshire who had settled in Rhode Island in 1640, when America was still a British colony, and started a commercial farm. His daughter, born on the voyage over, was given the poetic name Seaborn. Several generations later, one of his great-grandsons joined those who took up arms against England and paid with his life: in 1782 Captain Henry Tew was purported to have died on the infamous British prisoner ship the HMS *Jersey*.

Later, research would indicate that the captain in question had never existed, and Allene would be struck off the membership list. But at the time, the Pittsburgh branch of the DAR's research didn't reach that far. Energetic, wealthy members were needed, and the application was accepted. With this, Allene took her first step on the path to the respectability she had lost so radically by getting pregnant out of wedlock and eloping with her lover.

In the meantime, it slowly began to dawn upon Tod's mother that her new daughter-in-law was more than just a pretty face with an excess of ambition. Allene was strong and cheerful and precisely the anchor her charming but still stormy and, in essence, completely irresponsible son needed. What's more, Tod was and remained head over heels for his wife and little daughter and more or less functioned, in any case in the eyes of the outside world, as a respectable member of the management of the family business.

Allene and Tod spent the summer of 1892 again in their own Jimtown, where the sailing club was rebaptized the Conanicut Yacht Club and given its own accommodation in the form of a clubhouse financed by Tod, complete with a mooring jetty and a map room on the first floor. That fall, Allene became pregnant for the second time. Shortly thereafter, Tod's mother put aside her pride and moved back into her old house. As if to emphasize to the outside world that Tod's wife was now a proper member of the family, Rosetta and her daughter applied several years later for membership in the Daughters of the American Revolution.

***

For decades, Americans had been able to bask in the casual ease of their ever-growing affluence, but this changed from one day to the next in February 1893, when some alarming articles appeared in the newspapers. As a consequence of an economic depression in Europe, investors, especially British ones, were selling their overseas shares, particularly those in American railways, en masse, which drove down share prices. As a result, American banks began to get into difficulty, and the United States tumbled into a depression that would ultimately result in the bankruptcy of fifteen thousand businesses, of which seventy-four were railway companies and six hundred were banks.

The Panic of 1893, as this serious economic depression was called, made it painfully clear how dependent the young country actually was on foreign capital. But even more painful was the way it showed how completely amoral and unscrupulous Wall Street had become. Large commercial banks such as J.P. Morgan had implemented all kinds of practices and tricks to manipulate share value. There was no governmental control or legislation, and there was no one cheated investors could turn to because even judges allowed themselves to be paid off by the omnipotent banking sector.

As often was the case, it wasn't the instigators of the crisis who received the hardest knocks. No, it was the working class, and especially the hundred thousand unemployed. There wasn't any work, there were no benefits, there wasn't a single form of relief; for these people, the American dream had degenerated into a nightmare from which there was no escape.

The millionaires, on the other hand, partied and spent money as though nothing was wrong. Mrs. Astor had already lost her battle against the new money and accompanying bad taste that had flooded New York. Her nineteenth-century old New York, with its painterly streets, sober brownstones, and romantic gas lamps, was ousted by the noisy glitter and glamour of the nouveaux riches who moved to the city from all over America to show off their fortunes.

On Fifth Avenue in particular, pseudo-Gothic constructions, fake châteaus, and sham palazzos shot up out of the ground like dragon's teeth, each larger and more gaudy than the next. The houses were stuffed with artworks that had been pillaged from all over Europe and transported back to America by the shipload. It was rumored that the immensely rich newspaper magnate William Randolph Hearst needed two warehouses to store all of the old-world possessions he had amassed. Young, extravagant millionaires like Alva Vanderbilt, Mamie Fish, and Tessie Oelrichs outdid each other with parties that, it seemed, couldn't be expensive or bizarre enough, such as masquerade balls with themes like Roman orgies or French court dances. And if that wasn't enough to amuse the guests, you could always, as Mamie Fish once did, have a dressed-up monkey act as guest of honor.

The excesses and exorbitant extravagances of the superrich were widely reported in tabloid papers like the *New York Herald* and *Town Topics*. Young America was obsessed with money, and the general public was so insatiable for details of the lives, houses, and parties of the rich that a headline like "Rich Woman Falls Down Stairs—Not Hurt" could easily make the front page.

***

The Hostetters, too, didn't suffer in the least from the financial crisis. Their thinly veiled alcohol trade flourished, in fact, if only because the poor needed the solace of the herbal elixir more now than ever before and were prepared to spend their very last cent on it if necessary. This indifference to the crisis was reflected in Tod's spending habits. In October 1893, when most of America was in the grip of financial uncertainty, he commissioned yacht builder Herreshoff to design for him a new, more luxurious, and even bigger sailboat.

The *Duquesne* was more than 130 feet long and cost $50,000. The boat was so imposing that even the snobs at the New York Yacht Club could no longer ignore it. Under the pressure of the financial crisis, they had already been forced to reappraise their norms regarding respectability. Now they accepted Tod as a member and granted the *Duquesne* a permanent mooring berth in their New York marina.

A month later Tod bought a piece of land near a fork in the Beaver River, about thirty miles north of Pittsburgh, for $25,000. A year earlier he had purchased nearly 250 acres in the same place because his young wife just couldn't get used to the dirty air in Pittsburgh and longed for greenery and space.

Naid's Delight, as Tod's new property had been known, was described in 1770 by George Washington himself as "a good body of land." It was beautifully situated on a small tributary of the Ohio River called Raccoon Creek. Still used as farmland, it was perfect for the luxurious hunting lodge the young millionaire couple had built on it. Decades later, workmen would still remember how generous and friendly their employer had been. He was, in the words of one of them, "a first-class fellow to work for," with "few worries in life."

On October 6, 1894, the *Pittsburgh Press* published a detailed article about Hostetter House, as the hunting lodge was called. According to the article, the house resembled a gigantic log cabin, once more showing that Allene wasn't ashamed of her roots. She and Tod had been inspired by a building they'd seen the previous year in Chicago, during the first major world's fair to be held on American soil. The California State Building resembled a Spanish-style country house, incorporating different woods characteristic of all the states.

But the log cabin—only the chimney was built of brick—was one the pioneers could never have dreamed of. The house had a total of twenty-five rooms, including an impressive dining-and-ballroom and a just-as-fine sitting room. In the basement there were wine cellars and other storage rooms but also apartments built for the eight servants who lived there year-round. Along the river, space had been cleared for their own jetty, from which a drive lined with stately poplars led to the house. Next to the house was a polo field and a nine-hole golf course and beyond that, a stone house for the estate manager, kennels for a pack of hounds, and three large stable blocks. These contained Tod's favorite carriage, a tally-ho pulled by six horses, and—Allene's pride and joy—no fewer than forty chestnut horses for riding.

The whole thing had cost about $100,000, and the *Pittsburgh Press* was lyrical in its description. The article's headline read "Picturesque Raccoon Farm—A Country House of Magnificence where Wealth and Good Taste Are Combined to Produce the Happiest Effect." Now Pittsburgh society could no longer ignore the young Mrs. Hostetter, who had carved herself a way into an environment that had originally greeted her with cold hostility. From 1895 onward, Mrs. T. R. Hostetter and her two daughters—the younger, Verna, was born in January 1893—were given their own mention in the *Pittsburgh and Allegheny Blue Book*. This meant that scarcely four years after her much-discussed wedding, the girl from Jamestown had succeeded in conquering first her in-laws and then the elite of one of the richest cities in America.

3

The Lucky Plunger

At what point would Allene start to suspect that there was something seriously wrong with her husband? That his fascination for every opportunity that permitted betting or gambling—poker games, horse races, dogfights, boxing matches—was more than a youthful indulgence he would grow out of as he matured and took on the responsibilities of a family? And that Tod's restlessness—"He never sat still," according to a stable boy—could not be tempered by either her love for him or his for her? That, on the contrary, it would become ever worse and eventually be his downfall?

She'd later tell a friend that the turning point came in the fall of 1895, shortly after Verna, their younger daughter, had fallen ill and died, tragically, on her sister Greta's fourth birthday. Even Allene seemed to get over it fairly quickly. Death among babies and toddlers was quite common in those times—more than half of children died before their fifth year. For this reason, doctors often advised young parents not to get too attached to their children in the early years. What's more, Allene and Tod were still young, and many more children were certain to come.

But for Tod, little Verna's death was one too many. Perhaps this was because his childhood had been overshadowed by the early deaths of two older brothers—the first died at age twenty-three from an infection he'd contracted on a grand tour of Europe; the second died at seventeen of a contagious disease—and also by the premature death of his father, with whom Tod had been very close. And now he had to bury his two-year-old daughter, too, in the family plot high in the hills of Allegheny Cemetery, while there was nothing urgent or essential in his life to distract him from his grief.

The latter situation was, of course, the basis for Tod's restlessness. A fellow heir to a fortune, William K. Vanderbilt, would once comment with a remarkable display of self-knowledge how difficult life was when your father had achieved everything humanly possible and had left you, despite his millions, without any space to do anything meaningful yourself. "Inherited wealth is a real handicap to happiness," he said. "It is as certain death to ambition as cocaine is to morality."

***

In the winter of 1895–1896, Tod met the man who would become his nemesis, David "Davy" C. Johnson. This native New Yorker had his own private racing stables, several gambling houses, and a reputation as one of the most legendary gamblers on the continent. When Tod met him, Davy was thirty-nine; his death fifteen years later would be commemorated in the *New York Times* with a mixture of awe and amazement:

> You may talk about your plungers and betting men . . . but this country has never produced another such a man. He had played the game ever since he was ten years old and he met his losses with a smile. Defeat never found him despondent. His

coolness when thousands were at stake was wonderful. He appeared oftentimes to be the least
interested in the results when another man in his
position would have been driven by the uncertainty
to the verge of insanity . . . Johnson was probably
the most venturesome gambler who ever operated
on the American turf. It was no unusual thing for
him to bet up to 50,000 dollars on an event and
on what he was wont to call a dull afternoon, his
custom was to toss a cent for stakes of 1,000 dollars a side.

Soon Tod was spending more and more time with his older friend
in New York, which, thanks to the influence of new money, had grown
into the only place in North America that could measure up to the
big European cities in terms of influence and appearance. The leading
travel-guide series Baedeker printed in 1893: "It is the wealthiest city of
the New World, and inferior in commercial and financial importance
to London alone among the cities of the globe."

At first Tod would stay on the *Duquesne* in the New York Yacht
Club marina during these trips, but when fellow members began to
complain about the all-too-frequent presence of the not particularly
socially acceptable Johnson, he rented a four-story mansion, complete
with stables, at 12 East Sixty-Fifth Street. The house was walking distance from the Waldorf Astoria hotel, where Johnson inhabited a suite,
and the clubs of Broadway, where the duo were known as "high roll-
ers"—men for whom no challenge was too great.

Tod proved to be just as cool a player as, if not cooler than, his
friend—"the nerviest gentleman player," in the words of a New York
evening paper. He accepted losses with a shrug; when he won, he'd treat
everybody, or he'd give away his winnings to passing newspaper delivery
boys. His luck was legendary, particularly with horse racing. Although

he gave the impression of picking winners from thin air, the staff of restaurants he frequented later told journalists that he actually carefully studied previous results before laying his bets. He soon earned himself a name in gambling circles: the Lucky Plunger.

As Tod triumphed in his new role on Broadway, the country around him sank deeper and deeper into a seemingly endless economic recession. The contrast between the small group of elites who had ended up on the right side and the innumerable have-nots who had ended up on the wrong side of the American dream was very depressing by now—and all the more depressing because the instigators of the Panic of '93, and with it all of the misery most Americans were suffering, were counted among that former group.

In liberal circles especially, more and more questions were being asked about the unbridled capitalism that had counted as a form of evangelicalism in the United States up to then. Characteristic is an article in the *New York Times* from July 12, 1896, which reports the departure of Tod's *Duquesne* and several other expensive yachts for the New York Yacht Club's annual cruise. The yacht club cruise was the undisputed high point of the sailing season. An armada of hundreds of sailing yachts would slowly make its way into the more than hundred mile Long Island Sound while participants entertained themselves with races, regattas, and parties. It was said that you could walk across the champagne corks to the other side the morning after the fleet had moored in a harbor. For a duty reporter from the *New York Times*, the departure was a good opportunity to point out the extreme dichotomy in the America of those days:

> Several steam yachts were anchored off East 26th Street early in the morning and the scene on and around the dock of the Department of Correction was a gay one. Carriages were continually driving

up with jolly parties, who were taken out to the
yachts in naphtha launches or cutters.

In the midst of this gay scene the steamboat
Thomas E. Brennan arrived from Blackwell's Island
with about fifty unfortunate men and women who
had served a term on the island for some misde-
meanor and were brought ashore to be released.
They filed down one side of the dock and presented a picture in sad contrast to the other. On
one side were men strong, rich and happy, and
women handsome, well dressed and about to go
on some of the finest yachts of the world.

That same summer, a populist Democratic candidate had a serious
chance of getting into the White House. William Jennings Bryan promised social reform and to tackle the widespread corruption and greed
that had plunged the country into ruin. But at the last moment, entrepreneurs and the financial establishment, supported by the Presbyterian
Church, launched an aggressive countercampaign in which they told
the public that phenomena such as socialism and trade unions were
precisely what formed the greatest threat to what was left of the nation's
prosperity.

On November 3, 1896, the Republican candidate, William
McKinley, won the race. And so the rich continued to throw parties and
the poor suffered—although with increasing complaints and protests.
When a New York society couple, in the middle of the coldest winter
of the crisis, announced in 1897 the biggest, most expensive ball ever
organized in the city—for eight hundred guests, two entire stories of the
Waldorf Astoria would be transformed into the court of Versailles to the
tune of $400,000—they were subjected to the full force of the people's
anger. But none of the critical articles, angry reactions, or even death

threats could sway the couple, the Bradley-Martins, from their plans, and the offending ball was held on February 10. As if to demonstrate how untouchable they felt and how little they cared about the anger of the plebs or the misery in which their less fortunate fellow citizens lived, the host opened the ball by playing the well-known ditty "When You Ain't Got No Money, You Need Not Come Around."

By now the so-called yellow press, the gutter press, had developed a taste for pillorying the multimillionaires. William Waldorf Astor, heir to the hotel fortune, felt so threatened by the increasingly aggressive press hounds that he fled to Europe, hoping to find more respect and restraint toward the leisure class to which he belonged as a consequence of his birth. Unfortunately, inventions like the telegraph and the telephone meant that news now traveled faster across the ocean than he could. What's more, the English gutter press was just as vicious as New York's. As a consequence, Astor saw his comings and goings subjected to close scrutiny on both sides of the ocean, and he had even less room to maneuver than he'd had before.

At this time, Tod Hostetter was still just a small fish to the newspapers, a foolish young millionaire from Pittsburgh with poor taste in friends. The 1896 presidential election so important to the country was interesting to him because it was something he could bet on. Here, too, his legendary luck didn't let him down: he was the only person to guess all of the results correctly, down to the last decimal point, and won $30,000 in one blow. He lost the sum almost immediately on roulette, the only game of chance he lost time after time. In the words of a friend:

> Roulette was his ruin . . . He was the wildest plunger I ever knew, and he was smart as a steel trap, except when he played roulette. If he had left the wheel alone, he could not have lost anything, but he could not leave it alone. He was sure he would win in the end.

***

Allene did what she could to keep her husband away from the company of Davy Johnson and the temptations of horse racing and roulette. ("If one has the will and persistence, one CAN do things.") She turned Hostetter House on Raccoon Creek into the setting for "many a gay nineties party," it was later written. For years, local inhabitants would remember festively decorated boats filled with happy guests sailing to and from Pittsburgh. Allene also successfully threw her feminine charms into the battle, and in the early spring of 1897, she discovered she was pregnant again.

On October 2, 1897, Allene gave birth to a son, baptized Theodore Rickey Jr. after his father. Little Teddy, as the child was called to differentiate him from his father, Tod, originally seemed to have been born under a lucky star. A few months after his birth, America, its own fight for independence fresh in its memory, chose to side with the rebels in the Spanish colony of Cuba and went to war against Spain. This meant that little Teddy's father would have his first—and, as it would transpire, his only—chance to actually do something for his country. Tod put his *Duquesne* at the disposal of the American marines. It was therefore partly thanks to him that the Americans were able to drill the Spanish fleet in the Philippines into the ground on May 1, 1898.

The old superpower Spain turned out to be no match for the modern, patriotism-inspired America, and within a few months, America had won the Spanish-American War.

For the first time in its existence, the United States had manifested itself as an independent, imperial entity. During peace negotiations, the country even managed to gain Puerto Rico and the Philippines as colonies. Cuba became an American protectorate, and Hawaii was simply annexed: the leap to political world power had been more than successful.

The quickly won war gave a substantial boost to national self-confidence and was a blessing to the economy, which, as a consequence of the war efforts, quickly picked up speed again. But while his mother country climbed back out of her depression, Tod seemed to have gone too far downhill to be able to find his way back up again. The *Duquesne* returned to New York, and Tod resumed his career as a professional gambler with renewed élan. As the *Pittsburgh Press* would euphemistically summarize: "Theodore Hostetter was best-known for his devotion to sports."

In practice, this meant Tod belonged to the so-called Waldorf Crowd, an illustrious group of gamblers to which steel magnate Henry Clay Frick and industrialist John W. "Bet-a-Million" Gates also belonged. Gates was known for betting between poker games on such things as the route certain raindrops would take on the windows of his expensive hotel. Tod was in no way inferior to Gates in terms of creativity in gambling. If a fly landed on the table, he'd bet on which direction it would take off. If he saw a waiter coming over, he'd lay money on whether or not he'd drop his tray. And if he saw a beggar on the street, he'd bet on whether, if he gave him a hundred-dollar bill, he'd thank him profusely or make a swift getaway.

"If one has no steady belief and foundation to one's life, it is all hopelessness and tears," Allene would later write, clearly from personal experience. Tod had no belief or foundation in his life, and the hopelessness and tears were her own. After a while, she gave up organizing parties: the chance was great that her husband wouldn't be there, and his absence would only raise more embarrassing questions. She wasn't invited anywhere herself much, either. "Society, always fearful of Tod's wild ways, never bothered much about his pretty young wife," a journalist acquaintance would later write. Her hard-fought place among the Pittsburgh social elite would ultimately do her no good at all.

More and more often, the young Mrs. Hostetter was spotted with her children in the "log cabin" that had been built with so much pleasure on Raccoon Creek. She taught Teddy to ride and practiced with Greta for days on end on the obstacle course next to the house. Or she'd trot along on her horse, completely alone, spending hours in the dark woods around them. The glittering paradise she'd married into, and which she'd had all kinds of dreams about, had turned into a lonely place.

In the spring of 1901, Tod bought a new yacht. The *Seneca* was a whopping 330 feet long and had both a player piano and a roulette wheel below deck so that he could receive and entertain his gambling friends on the boat. He also bought an automobile, a "self-driving" car, the latest rage among the rich in those years. It was just "a small affair with no top," in the words of a servant, but small and open topped as it was, the car ensured that Tod was no longer dependent on the availability of horses, coachmen, or trains to New York. And that he could escape the watchful eyes of his wife and family whenever he wanted.

Allene and her children joined him on the *Seneca* that summer of 1901. But Tod barely saw them: he was below deck day and night playing roulette with his friends. At a certain point, Allene must have realized that even with all the will and persistence in the world, she still wouldn't be able to compete with the demons that had taken possession of Tod. And neither would love. She left the yacht and her husband and traveled with her children to her in-laws' at Narragansett Pier. Greta was nine when her mother officially divorced her father, and Teddy was just four. Their parents' marriage had lasted ten years.

***

Later it would be estimated that Tod went through an average of nearly $100,000 a month during that last winter. He cut "one of the widest swaths of the sporting fraternity," as the *Washington Post* would later write with fitting understatement. The fact that his brother Herbert had become the trustee of his funds after Allene left him didn't hold him back at all. He simply borrowed money from Davy Johnson, who had him sign IOU after IOU, one friend to another.

Canfield's Club became Tod's regular hangout. It was a casino that had opened in 1899 on Forty-Fourth Street, right next to the world-famous Delmonico's restaurant and opposite the chic Sherry Hotel. Its owner, Richard Canfield, had been a porter at the prestigious Union Club in a former life and knew exactly what men with too much money and too few challenges needed in their lives. His club breathed luxury and privacy, whether for men who wanted a place to take women they weren't married to or for millionaires wanting to try their luck with baccarat or at the roulette table.

A New York newspaper would later write expressively, "Canfield's was the scene of many a wastrel heir's downfall." Among the wastrel heirs were two grandsons of Cornelius Vanderbilt. One of them managed to lose $120,000 in a single evening, while his cousin Reginald "Reggie" Claypoole Vanderbilt managed to amass gambling debts of more than $400,000 in the space of six months. And then of course there was Tod, the young Pittsburgher who drowned his sorrows about his failed marriage and lost life evening after evening, and at the end of an evening would sign any paperwork put before him.

Tod was not present on Allene's thirtieth birthday, July 7, 1902. She spent the day with her children at her in-laws' at Narragansett Pier. Earlier that year she had rented a small house on East Seventy-Third Street as a New York pied-à-terre for herself and her parents, who had come over from Jamestown to support their daughter through these difficult times. She also sought consolation and distraction in her horses. She garnered high praise on August 21 with what the *New York Times* described as a "handsome pair of piebald ponies" during Narragansett Pier's first horse show.

In the meantime, Tod made half-hearted attempts to make amends with his family and wife between bouts of gambling. On July 30, he sailed the *Seneca* to the Larchmont Yacht Club's harbor to visit his brother Herbert. His breathlessness on this occasion was put down to his weight—he was short and had always tended toward plumpness, but by now he was simply fat. That evening, at the Waldorf Astoria, he complained of a cold, which he believed he'd caught that day on board his ship.

On Friday, two days later, he paid a short visit to the *Duquesne*, where he gave his steward instructions for the installation of a new roulette wheel to be placed the following day. Saturday night he spent at his house on East Sixty-Fifth Street, playing poker with friends. As usual, the game was played with great enthusiasm, and when the host became dangerously short of breath around midnight, no one thought to fetch a doctor.

And so the Lucky Plunger died in the early morning of the third day of August, of what would later be diagnosed as a neglected case of pneumonia, among the playing cards and friends who weren't friends and, ultimately, entirely alone. He was only thirty-two years old.

***

Tod's body was taken by train to his birthplace the next night. Allene, who had rushed from Rhode Island to New York that morning, was with her parents at East Seventy-Third Street. The next morning, when the printers' ink announcing the death of the young Pittsburgh million-aire in the newspapers was barely dry, casino owner Richard Canfield knocked on her door. He presented the astonished widow with a pile of promissory notes amounting to more than a quarter of a million dollars.

The funeral took place on Tuesday, August 5. For most of the day, Tod's body, surrounded by wildflowers, was laid out in the reception hall of his sister's house on Western Avenue. In the afternoon, the ser-vice was held there, too. The attendance was overwhelming. Whatever his weaknesses may have been, Tod had always been generosity and cheerfulness themselves and had never harmed a fly.

At the end of the afternoon, Tod was laid to rest next to his brothers, his father, and his little daughter in the Allegheny Cemetery. His coffin was carried by childhood friends, including the nephews of steel magnate Andrew Carnegie and train tycoon Joshua Rhodes—young men who, unlike him, hadn't succumbed under the weight of too much money and their fathers' successes.

***

At first, the Hostetter family successfully managed to keep the circumstances surrounding the death of the family's black sheep out of the press. According to the official line, he was said to have died in a sanatorium on Park Avenue of an unspecified illness. The papers managed to get wind of the story in the winter of 1903 thanks to Davy Johnson, who launched a court case against Tod's heirs on January 20 of that year. At stake was a sum of $115,000 that he claimed to have won from Tod during his favorite game of flipping coins.

Coincidentally or not, the New York police raided Canfield's Club that same day and arrested the business manager. The charge was that on the night of April 15, 1902, the manager had deliberately gotten the young Hostetter drunk in order to have him sign a promissory note of $30,000. Earlier attempts to close the famous casino—in particular after the young Vanderbilts suffered painful losses—had failed. But this time it worked. The detectives from the metropolitan police force ascertained that Canfield's employed large-scale deceit: trick wheels, fake faro card layouts, and "false and clogged dice." The club's death warrant had been signed.

The raid on Forty-Fourth Street also meant the end of the hope that Tod's pitiful death could be kept out of the public eye. On February 8, 1903, the *New York Times* opened with the headline "Theodore Hostetter—'The Lucky Plunger'—Lost a Million in a Year." According to the story, papers left behind showed that at the time of his death Tod owed Davy Johnson a massive $620,000. Aside from this, he was said to have $300,000 outstanding at Canfield's and other casinos, which brought his total debt to nearly $1 million.

The next day, speaking through his lawyer, Richard Canfield denied any involvement or even having known Tod. Davy Johnson, on the other hand, gave interviews to just about any journalist who came knocking. He said that his lawyers had instigated the case in Pittsburgh without his knowledge and that he'd suspended it as soon as he heard. It was unsporting to settle gambling debts in the courts, he said. He seemed genuinely shocked by the death of his young friend:

> I loved Tod. He was the best sport I have ever seen. I regret the publicity that rose out of this matter on account of the widow and children of "Tod" Hostetter. I believe that Mrs. Hostetter will say that I always treated her husband on the level, that I was his sincere friend, that I liked him personally and that I was of more value than expense to him when it is considered what a wild plunger he was. But it is hard to keep track of a man who would bet $1,000 a game on polo at Narragansett Pier.

A few weeks later, Johnson would announce that his racing stables were for sale and that he was quitting any kind of betting for good. He had settled any claims on Tod Hostetter's legacy behind closed doors.

Ultimately, Johnson was as unable to cope with life without betting as his dead friend had been: eight years later he would die the inveterate gambler he'd always been. In one newspaper, his obituary was given the befitting headline "Famous Plunger Accepts Last Bet."

As for Tod's pretty young widow, as the *Evening World* called Allene, she wisely held her tongue. It seems that after his death, Allene didn't stay a day longer than necessary in the city she'd called her home for more than eleven years but where she'd never felt truly welcome. She left behind her husband and youngest daughter in their hillside graves, she left behind the Hostetter clan with its veiled alcohol empire, and she left behind Pittsburgh with its black clouds of smoke. She took her son and daughter with her and left via the same route she'd come in 1891, only now in the opposite direction, from Pittsburgh to New York.

And she never looked back.

4

New York, New York

If Allene had been searching for a suitable anthill to disappear into, she couldn't have thought of a better place than Empire City, as New York now proudly nicknamed itself. Four years earlier, Manhattan had combined with its surrounding districts, including Queens and Brooklyn, and the city with 3.5 million inhabitants had become the largest in the world after London. And it was still an unrivaled magnet for immigrants: on some days, the border post on Ellis Island welcomed no fewer than twenty-one thousand newcomers.

Manhattan had grown into a physical symbol of what human ingenuity and energy could achieve. The deployment of steel construction and the "safety hoister"—the elevator—meant that buildings were growing ever taller, with the twenty-two-story Flatiron Building counting as the provisional high point in 1902. The once-so-dark Broadway became a "Great White Way" where the general public feasted its eyes day and night on the giant floodlit shop windows of exclusive department stores and boutiques—this thanks to the invention of a "small ball of sunlight, a true Aladdin's lamp": Thomas Edison's light bulb.

Some writers, such as Edith Wharton and Henry James, emigrated to Europe, disgusted by the raw concrete, harsh light, and vulgarity of industrialized America; other writers and artists were drawn en masse to the most modern and lively and least bourgeois city in the world. In the words of writer Charles Eliot Norton:

> This is a wonderful city. There is a special fitness in the first syllable of its name, for it is essential New and seems likely always to remain so. The only old things here are yesterday's newspapers.

Pedestrians, carriages, horse-drawn carts, donkey carts, and cyclists fought for a place in the streets with automobiles, omnibuses, and the electric streetcars that had been deployed as public transport since 1900. The smell of horse dung mixed with exhaust fumes, and everywhere horns were tooted, bells were rung, and voices were raised, with, above it all, the screaming of the "els"—the elevated trains that ran along the entire length of Manhattan and were intended to reduce the chaos but somehow only managed to add to it.

Allene experienced herself just how dangerous the confrontation between old and new could be on May 14, 1903, when an omnibus so frightened the horses pulling the carriage she was in that they bolted. Both horses and passengers escaped with just shock, but because of these kinds of accidents and the alarming number of traffic fatalities, that year work was begun on an underground train tunnel that would grow into the New York subway network.

There was no city more hospitable and none more capricious than New York, with her "pull-down-and-build-all-over-again spirit," as poet Walt Whitman succinctly put it. Now that automobiles were rendering horse stables superfluous and it was becoming easier to commute between country house and city, luxurious apartment complexes were becoming increasingly popular.

The big, fancy town houses the nouveaux riches had recently built to withstand all eternity fell prey to wrecking balls, one by one. In most cases, their interiors, bought in Europe along with priceless art objects of great historical value, ended up in the trash heap. In answer to the question of whether they couldn't be preserved, one demolition contractor summarized the mood in New York in those days with "I don't deal in secondhand goods."

In retrospect, Tod had literally gambled himself to death at nearly the same moment that the period his life unintentionally symbolized came to an end. While in the spring of 1903 the newspapers were still full of stories about his gambling mania, a new wave of public indignation was welling. Its new target: the eccentric Chicago industrialist C. K. G. Billings, who had rented out a floor of the Sherry Hotel to stage a dinner for thirty-six costumed guests on horseback. This time, public opinion was too powerful for big money: the dinner went ahead but at a different, strictly confidential location, and the Billings Horseback Dinner went down in history as one of the death throes of the Gilded Age.

The frenzied hedonism and absurd luxury that had given the last decade of the nineteenth century its gaudy overtone simply went out of fashion. Even such a spoiled society doyenne as Alva Belmont was searching for a better way to give her life meaning, joining the suffragette movement. At the same time, the filthy rich had become less filthy and less rich, thanks to the young politician Theodore Roosevelt, who had succeeded as president after McKinley was assassinated in 1901. Roosevelt may have been a Republican, but he was a lot more sensitive to the changing times than his predecessor. He started regulating banks, the food industry, and railway trusts; introduced higher taxes; and for the first time consulted the trade unions, which the government had looked upon with suspicion up to then.

The changing times had an effect on the lives of the Hostetters, too. Both tax authorities and prohibitionists had firmly set their sights on the family's bitters empire, and in some places, pharmacists who still dared to sell the controversial herb drink as a medicine were prosecuted. In 1905, Hostetter's Bitters was officially added to the list of alcoholic drinks and taxed as such.

Greta and Teddy Hostetter inherited what was left of Tod Hostetter's possessions, including the hunting lodge at Raccoon Creek, but they no longer received the annual Niagara Falls' worth of dollars to which their father had succumbed. As far as Allene was concerned, she seemed not to have inherited anything except her husband's personal gambling debts and a last name that had been dragged through the mud. Her brother-in-law Herbert, with whom she'd never really gotten along, was in charge of the settlement of Tod's estate and of his children's inheritance.

This meant that for every important decision, Allene had to go to her detested Pittsburgh. If she was so keen to live in New York, she'd have to make do with her barely twenty-foot-wide rental house on Seventy-Third Street. When her former mother-in-law died in the summer of 1904 at the age of seventy-five, Allene didn't get a cent. The $5 million Rosetta left behind was shared out among her one remaining son, her daughter, and Tod's children.

***

There was only one way in which a woman without profession or means could take her life in a new direction in those days, and that was through a man. And Allene found one—and incredibly quickly, too. On August 28, 1904, at the third annual Narragansett horse show, Allene showed herself in public for the first time with the New York stockbroker Morton Nichols, the man who was to become her second husband.

Nichols was a dream partner, at least on paper. He was the youngest son of the wealthy gold merchant William Snowden Nichols, who had worked on the New York Stock Exchange for more than fifty years and counted as one of the country's most important authorities on financial matters. With his dark blond curls and blue eyes, Morton wasn't unattractive, although his chin was described on his passport application as "not heavy"—which, in the thinking of the times, might have been seen as a sign of a weak character. Aside from this, he also had the reputation for being rather surly and not keen to marry.

A society magazine had characterized him early that summer as follows:

> Morton Colton Nichols is one of the club bachelors who is seen a great deal in society. Mr. Nichols is a member of the Metropolitan Club, which he practically makes his home. He was graduated from Harvard in 1892. Besides the Metropolitan he belongs to the Union League, the Racquet, and the University. He is a stock broker and comes from an old New England family. He is currently one of the house party staying with Mr. and Mrs. Reginald C. Vanderbilt at Newport.

Indeed, Morton, who was thirty-four years old when he met Allene, had until that moment shown little sign of a burning need to give up his comfortable life in the gentlemen's clubs for the commitments of marriage. He had been engaged to Vivian Sartoris, the pretty British granddaughter of former president Ulysses S. Grant, for more than five years, with some gaps. However, that had never resulted in marriage, and in 1903 she'd married somebody else.

Morton's lightning romance with Allene seems to have mainly come about under pressure from his eighty-two-year-old father, who had recently been diagnosed with an incurable form of cancer. His two eldest sons were literally and figuratively taken care of: they worked for him in the family business and had been respectably married for years.

William Nichols was therefore keen to guide his until-then rather directionless youngest son into a safe harbor before his death. The *New York Times* later wrote that the elderly gold merchant had begged Allene to marry his son so that he could be there.

The wedding took place on December 27, 1904, at Saint Thomas Church in London, in private—this, it was claimed, was because of Morton's father's physical state. The fact that the ceremony took place on the other side of the ocean suggests that those concerned were doing their best to keep this notable union between the proverbial eternal bachelor and the widow with a tale as far from the searchlights of the press as possible.

Nevertheless, a British correspondent for the *Washington Post* managed to gather a few interesting details, such as the fact that Morton didn't arrive at the church until the very last minute. According to the official statement, he hadn't wanted to leave his father's sickbed.

***

This was how Allene started the year 1905: freed from the gold-plated headlock of the Hostetters, free, too, from the name that had gained such negative connotations. Through her connection to the Nicholses—a Mrs. Astor–approved American blue-book family, she and her children now automatically belonged to the highest echelons of society. And though neither Teddy nor Greta was ever formally adopted by their stepfather, they quietly continued life with his last name.

After a short honeymoon in Canada, in early 1905, the family moved into a temporary residence on East Seventy-Sixth Street while they waited for their own house to be built. This was one of Allene's conditions. She'd had her fill of living in houses belonging to her in-laws.

In the meantime and against all expectations, the elderly William Nichols managed to cling to life for another six months. He died on July 23, 1905, leaving his sons millions. Two weeks later, Morton applied for a passport for a lengthy world tour he wanted to go on with his new family. The trip would take more than a year. He was, according to the application, a retired banker now. Clearly he'd quit his job at the J.P. Morgan commercial bank right after his father's death.

Allene met these travel plans with open arms—if she hadn't, perhaps, come up with them herself. Not only would the round-the-world trip bridge the period until their new house would be completed, it also seemed the ideal way to work her second life partner free of his beloved clubs and the less desirable elements in his circle of friends. However different Tod and Morton were in character, they did have one thing in common: Morton, too, was no stranger to racecourses, and he kept up intimate friendships with dyed-in-the-wool gamblers. Reginald Vanderbilt, who had lost sums almost as astronomical as Tod had in Canfield's Club, counted among his friends, as did Joseph Ullman, the owner of a racing stables and the biggest bookmaker in America.

Transcontinental travel was all the rage among America's richest at the time. While the nineteenth-century elite had barely left their country—Tod Hostetter had never owned a passport—those in this exciting new century did little else. Large shipping companies like the White Star Line and the Cunard Line competed with each other in the size, speed, and luxuriousness of their majestic ocean liners. Some ships even had internal telephone connections on board.

That Allene's children would miss a part of their schooling was not considered a problem. A trip around the world would be good for their development and help them overcome the shocking events in their young lives. They had withstood their parents' divorce, their father's death and the scandal around it, the sudden move to New York, and, shortly after that, the sudden arrival of a total stranger who was their new father—although he showed little sign of considering them anything more than his wife's necessary baggage.

***

The Nichols family trip can easily be followed through the society columns, which were wont to keep the home front accurately informed about the comings and goings of the so-called Steamer Set. After boarding a ship in September, the family spent the winter in Asia, where they moored in Singapore and Batavia. In the spring, they visited Egypt. Next, they set sail for Europe for extended visits to London, Paris, and the French Riviera.

During this part of the journey, Allene had her parents brought over from New York. She bought them an apartment in Nice, where they could spend a peaceful old age in the mild weather of the South of France, as many Russian and European aristocrats had traditionally done.

The family continued on its travels, now to the American West Coast, where they stopped at Hawaii and Los Angeles, among other places. In the fall of 1906, they arrived back in New York, where they took up residence at 57 East Sixty-Fourth Street in their brand-new town house, which could already count itself among the prettiest and most elegant houses in the city.

The Allene Tew Nichols House, as the building was named after its patron, was designed by one of the most fashionable architects of the period, Charles "Cass" P. H. Gilbert. He had trained at the prestigious École des Beaux-Arts in Paris, and the cosmopolitan style that was in vogue, with its attention to symmetry and balance, fit him like a glove. The building he had built for Allene, with its pale gray stucco and curving facade, was seven stories tall and included a six-person elevator, seven fireplaces, and twelve bedrooms, each equipped with its own bathroom.

The progress of the couple's marriage in the meantime has not been documented, but the chances are that upon their return, Morton, a clubman at heart, immediately got back to nestling into the cozy leather armchairs and the equally cozy atmosphere of his men's clubs, as he had in the old days. He continued to give the Metropolitan Club as his postal address, in any case.

Allene, in turn, doesn't seem to have suffered from the absence of her rather uninspiring husband. She had a house to furnish, children to raise—fifteen-year-old Greta was enrolled at Miss Spence's School, an elite girls' school on the Upper West Side, and nine-year-old Teddy was given a private tutor—and a busy life on the New York social scene where she had to put in appearances. Soon Allene was known as a fantastic, inexhaustible organizer of primarily charity benefits, raising money for schools and hospitals and other worthy causes.

Not only was the young Mrs. Nichols good at organizing things, she could also entertain. Her talents—although she wouldn't have told this to the chic ladies with whom she was active on all kinds of committees—were thanks to her childhood in the old-fashioned immigrant town of Jamestown, which was rife with all kinds of superstitions brought over from Europe. She had learned clairvoyance and palm reading there and had already successfully amused fellow passengers with her skills during her round-the-world trip.

***

In the spring of 1906, California was hit by a severe earthquake and fire that took more than three thousand lives. The next year, Wall Street shook in its foundations; the stock market took an alarming nosedive, and a new financial crisis seemed inevitable. Once again, the panic could be attributed to a bubble in the market, a consequence of "financialization"—large institutions juggling with money. In this case, the main culprits were trusts. They were intended to manage family fortunes, but after President Roosevelt imposed restrictions on regular banks, they were being used as unregulated "pirate banks."

The first to collapse was the Knickerbocker Trust, which had been believed unassailable. After that, it was just a question of time before

others would follow—including The Manhattan Company, in which
the Nichols family's entire fortune was housed. Subsequently the entire
financial system was dragged down, just as it had been after the Panic of
1893. Anxious weeks followed, during which the American government
desperately tried to get enough money together to rescue the system and
save the country from a new catastrophe. The $25 million raised was put
in the hands of top banker J. P. Morgan, a.k.a. the Jupiter of Wall Street.

In early November, it became clear that Morton's former employer
had indeed managed to keep the trust afloat, and with it the financial
stability of the country. Share prices made their way back up again,
the population stopped holding its breath, and it was business as usual
again for New York's rich—perhaps with even more self-confidence
than before, because wasn't the Panic of 1907 ultimate proof that modern man could mold anything to his will, overcoming even the threat
of financial collapse?

What couldn't be contrived, though, however good the intentions
of both parties might have been, was a happy marriage. Allene and
Morton were seen together increasingly infrequently and rarely named
in newspaper columns. The last time was on November 11, 1908, as a
result of a burglary at the house on Sixty-Fourth Street, in which $1,500
worth of Greta's jewelry was stolen. Allene told a reporter that she'd
placed her own valuables in a safe before going to the theater with her
husband that evening.

Things became quiet around the couple after this never-solved
theft—Morton accused their Canadian butler, who was later proved
innocent—just as quiet as they had been during the later years of
Allene's marriage to Tod. The only member of the family to pop up
in the press briefly was her son, Teddy, and that was on September 30,
1909, the day New York got to see a flying machine for the first time.

The entire city had turned out to stare at the invention of Orville
and Wilbur Wright, two bicycle mechanics from Ohio. Their twin-
engine airplane made a lap around the Statue of Liberty before swooping

down over the RMS *Lusitania*, a British passenger ship on its way to Europe, to loud cheers from the crowds on the shore. At the same time, the many yachts anchored around the Statue of Liberty sounded their horns. One of those boats, according to a report in the *New York Times*, was the *Seneca*, owned by T. R. Hostetter Jr.

More surprising than the fact that Tod's extravagant craft was still in the family was the name by which its youthful owner was identified. After five years of going through life as Teddy Nichols, Allene's son was suddenly using the name of his biological father again.

***

During Allene's Victorian youth, divorce still counted as an ultimate deadly sin. But Queen Victoria had been dead and buried since 1901, and the period named after her—which included the rigid, overly prudish morals of the time—had become a thing of the past. In 1909, millionaires who wanted to end their marriages had more reason to fear the press—the self-appointed kings of the world—than the wrath of God or the disapproval of those around them.

For the muckrakers, as President Roosevelt had called the intrusive press corps three years earlier, reporting on a society divorce counted as the absolute pinnacle of their careers. Court records were public in America, so the unfortunates who appeared in the newspaper columns would see their private lives dissected to the last unsavory detail. This was why John Jacob "Jack" Astor, the son of Caroline Astor, did everything he could to end his famously unhappy marriage as quietly and inconspicuously as possible after his mother's death. When the press found out anyway, he was subjected to angry criticism and taunts in the newspapers for years on end.

Like many rich Americans, the Nichols couple resorted to a so-called Paris divorce. In France, court records weren't public. What's more, divorces there could be granted on the grounds of simple

infidelity, while in America that only counted if the extramarital affair
had taken place *in* the marital home. In that day and age, divorcées kept
their former husband's name, which helped keep a divorce hidden from
the outside world. When "Mrs. Morton C. Nichols" was extensively
photographed for the society pages of the *New York Times* in the spring
of 1909, she was in fact no longer that.

The photos show that Allene was still an exceptionally handsome
woman at the age of thirty-seven. But the challenging, spirited look
she'd had in her eye as a girl had totally disappeared. Two failed marriages in a row had taken their toll and taught her that while will and
persistence might have been enough for her pioneering predecessors to
create their own paradise, in her case, real life kept getting in the way
of her dreams and she would have to apply her persistence to making
the best of things yet again.

After the divorce, Morton seems to have disappeared completely
from the city for a while. From time to time, his name was mentioned
in connection with society parties in Palm Beach, a place in Florida
that the American elite had taken over as their new vacation paradise a
few years earlier. He didn't turn up again in New York until February
1911, surprisingly enough as the brand-new fiancé of a certain Ethel
Dietz. This debutante compensated for an obvious lack of physical
charms with her youthful years—she was seventeen years younger than
Morton—and the large fortune awaiting her as the sole grandchild of
hurricane lantern manufacturer R. E. Dietz.

A month after the engagement announcement in the paper, Allene
made an application to the New York courts, asking to take her first
husband's name again. She did not want to be confused with her former
husband's new wife, she claimed. The courts honored her request, and
when Greta and her classmates celebrated their high school graduation
on May 24, 1911, in the same ballroom of Sherry's where Billings had
wanted to give his infamous Horseback Dinner eight years earlier, both
she and her mother were using their old last name.

Allene might have seemed to be back to square one—but this wasn't entirely true. The details of her divorce may have been safely hidden away in the archives of the *tribunal de grande instance* in Paris, but the 1910 census shows that she learned a thing or two from the earlier collapse of the Hostetters' glittering paradise. According to documentation, in addition to being the head of a household that included seven servants and her two children, she was also the owner of the substantial house at 57 East Sixty-Fourth Street. She also owned another two houses on Park Avenue, numbers 604 and 606, which a rental agent managed for her.

Clearly the deal Allene had made five years earlier with the old gold dealer who had begged her to marry his son had been highly lucrative. "Her fortune was largely augmented by her alliance with the Nichols family," the *Washington Post* wrote later. Allene had become a businesswoman.

5

The Happy Island

Whatever had changed in high society at the beginning of the new century, one thing had stayed the same, and that was the importance of finding a suitable husband for a marriageable daughter. Allene had taken her chances and used them. Now, having celebrated her twentieth birthday in September 1911, it was Greta's turn.

Greta was fairly late to debut on the social scene: the average deb was sixteen or seventeen. At first glance, there would appear to be no reason for her not to have had a line of eager young suitors. She had inherited her father's dark good looks and his friendly, pleasant nature—though, like him, she was susceptible to a certain plumpness. From her mother, she had inherited striking blue eyes and great talent as a horsewoman. And she was rich. She and Teddy were the heirs to several million dollars, still carefully managed by their uncle Herbert.

Although the society sections report Greta's presence at plenty of parties for debutante friends and classmates, there was no question of making her debut herself, let alone becoming engaged. This probably had something to do with her mother, or rather with her mother's turbulent love life. If there was one thing the mothers of eligible young bachelors on the New York scene ran a mile from, it was that unfortunate combination of divorce and scandal. And those two things were present in abundance in the young life of the Lucky Plunger's daughter. Allene, never to be put off her stride, abandoned the snobs in New York for what they were and left for Europe with her daughter. In doing this, she was following in the footsteps of numerous American heiresses who, for whatever reasons, were considered less than marriageable in their own country. Dollar princesses, they were called, who, in exchange for an impressive-sounding title and its accompanying prestige, would buy their way into aristocratic families on the other side of the ocean. Around 1900, the British aristocracy counted more than five hundred Americans, and there was scarcely a distinguished family to be found that didn't have a daughter-in-law from the New World.

The English barons, lords, and counts had little choice: as a consequence of mechanization and the competition of cheap grain and meat from America, their own rural estates were earning less and less, while taxes were rising. They would even place personal ads in New York newspapers in which they'd announce—in so many words—their search for a moneyed wife. A woman's lack of status in her home country was something they accepted: for them, all Americans were equally socially unacceptable, and so, as the British writer Ruth Brandon pithily put it, "one might therefore pick the richest without compunction."

Some of these alliances worked out extremely well, such as in the case of Jennie Jerome, who married Lord Randolph Churchill in 1874 and became the mother of British prime minister Winston Churchill. The 1909 marriage of banker's widow Olive Grace Kerr, a good friend of Allene's, to the third Baron Greville was incredibly successful, too. "American women are bright, clever, and wonderfully cosmopolitan," Oscar Wilde opined. They often didn't just bring money but also welcome new blood and a breath of fresh air to the old castles.

Other fairy-tale weddings were less happy, such as that of Consuelo Vanderbilt, whose ambitious mother married her off to the Duke of

Marlborough in 1895. Just as unhappy was the beautiful, powerful, and
rich Mary Hasell, a friend of Greta's, who married British baron George
Borwick in 1908. It soon became clear to the new baroness that a title
and a collection of old family portraits offered no guarantee of marital
happiness. Her husband gambled, got into debt all over the place, and
saw the fact that he'd married his wife for her money as a reason to treat
her with as much scorn as possible. Sometimes, she admitted to Greta,
he even spat at her.

***

When Allene and Greta arrived in England in early June 1911, they
decided to take the unhappy Mary with them. In the fall, the three
women moved on to France, where Greta was the honored guest of the
Duchess d'Uzès in Rambouillet and, according to the *Washington Post's*
correspondent, widely admired for her riding skills. Next they traveled
to British India, where they took in the polo season and witnessed the
"durbar"—festivities to celebrate King George V's investiture as the
official emperor of the overseas territories.

Halfway through February 1912, the three women returned to
England. Mary Hasell found herself standing in front of a locked door
as access to her in-laws' London house was rudely denied her. She
moved into Claridge's hotel and began very public divorce proceedings
as revenge—this to the delight of the press hounds on both sides of the
ocean and, it seemed, even to Mary herself. Dressed up dramatically,
she made the most of every opportunity in the courts to glory in her
role as the tragic heroine.

Perhaps due to Mary's bad experiences—or perhaps during the
women's nine-month trawl through the British Empire no suitable
marriage candidates had announced themselves—Greta still wasn't
engaged when she and her mother returned to New York empty-handed

in mid-March 1912. Once there, Allene organized an official coming-out for her daughter, sparing no cost or effort.

The debutante's party took place on April 9, 1912, at Sherry's. More than a hundred guests were invited for the dinner alone, including Greta's many girlfriends, family members from Pittsburgh, and all kinds of friends and business relations of Allene's. A further hundred guests were invited to the after-dinner ball, held in a room lavishly decorated with fresh white and yellow spring flowers. Greta was radiant in white satin with pearls; her mother was stunning in dark blue satin with diamonds, and the *New York Times* gave a trusty account of what seemed to be a very promising debutante's ball in all respects, even if it was a little on the late side.

Less than a week later, any thought of high society and parties or the reporting thereof was wiped away with one blow by shocking reports that the brand-new deemed-unsinkable flagship of the White Star Line, the RMS *Titanic*, had hit an iceberg on its way to New York and sunk. Fewer than 700 of the more than 2,220 people on board survived. Among the victims were many prominent New Yorkers, such as steel magnate Benjamin Guggenheim, Macy's owner Isidor Straus, and John Jacob Astor. The papers had castigated Astor, a divorced man of forty-seven, for marrying an eighteen-year-old classmate of Greta's, but now "Colonel Astor" was exalted by the same papers as a heroic figure.

The psychological impact of the shipwreck on the night of April 14–15 was enormous. For years, people had imagined themselves more powerful than nature and trusted blindly in the wonders of technology—but now the same technology had proved fallible in a terrible manner, shaking people's view of the world. Many saw the wreck of the *Titanic* as an apocalyptic harbinger of greater disasters, punishment for modern man's arrogance and presumption. Even the always self-assured New York began to doubt itself.

There was little room in this climate for the worries of rich girls in search of husbands. Society parties were canceled for the time being

or kept as modest as possible. Greta's coming-out had hit the rocks—
thanks to the unsinkable *Titanic*. Yet the party at Sherry's at the end of
1912 did lead to a marriage—though not for the debutante herself but
for someone who, given her age and her past, would hardly have seemed
eligible for new love. Namely, her mother.

***

It wasn't a rich heir this time—not a big-city boy, either. There was no
impressive posh name, and he wasn't a gambler. If one had to devise
a husband in every way different from his predecessors, this was he.
Anson Wood Burchard was a calm, stable, self-made man who had
worked his way up entirely on his own strengths to become one of the
country's leading engineers. And engineers, as everybody knew, were
America's unsung heroes—the quiet motors behind the former colony's
transformation into one of the wealthiest countries in the world.

Anson's background resembled Allene's in many respects. He was
born and raised in a small town north of New York City, which, like
Jamestown, had blossomed during the Industrial Revolution. The man-
ufacture of agricultural implements had pushed Hoosick Falls toward
the march of progress—it was no coincidence the main road was called
Mechanic Street.

As a young child, Anson had absorbed a love of technology from
his surroundings. In 1881, at the age of sixteen, he went to study electri-
cal engineering at the best technical college in America at that time,
the Stevens Institute of Technology in New Jersey. After that he spent
almost twenty years at his childless uncle's furniture and steam engine
factory. The factory gave Anson all the space he needed to develop better
machines for industrial uses such as heating, ventilation, and plumbing.
After a brief adventure in Mexico—where he worked as the manager
of a copper mine—in 1901 he was taken on as financial officer at the
merely eight-years-old but already very promising General Electric on

the recommendation of his brother-in-law and childhood friend GE vice president Hinsdill Parsons.

GE was the brainchild of Charles Albert Coffin, a former shoe manufacturer who in 1892 had the idea of uniting the many private electricity companies in America at that time into one large national network. With support from the inventor Thomas Edison and banking tycoon J. P. Morgan, who financed the plans, he was able to create an internationally operational electricity group within a relatively short time.

Like many successful entrepreneurs, Coffin had a keen eye for talent, and the technical and financial abilities of the big, quiet man from Hoosick Falls didn't go unnoticed. Within a few years, Anson had risen in the ranks to Coffin's personal assistant. When Parsons died in a car crash in April 1912, Anson replaced him as vice president. Strangely enough, the accident took place just after the same Hinsdill Parsons dragged the still-unmarried Anson to the coming-out party of a certain Greta Hostetter.

In October, Anson went to Europe on a business trip. He was accompanied by his newly widowed sister and Edwin Rice, a brilliant engineer who had built up GE from its early days. Once they'd arrived in London, the trio took up residence in Claridge's. And by chance, acquaintances from New York were staying there, too—the widow Hostetter and her daughter.

That fall Teddy had started at an expensive boarding school near Boston, and Allene and Greta were in London "spending their time shopping and doing the theatres," according to the *New York Times*. But the glamour of the London department stores and theaters was clearly overshadowed by their new companions from General Electric—and in particular by the tall figure of its forty-seven-year-old vice president.

***

On November 22, 1912, the *New York Times* published a remarkable
story on its front page. GE senior official Anson Wood Burchard had
apparently requested a license to marry Mrs. Hostetter, "well known in
society," but had withdrawn it a few hours later. The duty correspondent
caught whiff of a romantic intrigue and posted himself in the lobby
of the hotel, determined to stay there until he knew exactly what was
going on.

"Widow Is Not Yet Certain" was the headline the paper ran later.
The industrious journalist had even managed to get a few words out of
Allene on the matter:

> In answer to a question as to whether she was
> going to marry Mr. Burchard, Mrs. Hostetter replied:
> "I don't know."
>
> When told that Mr. Burchard had applied for a
> license, fixing the event for Dec. 5, and afterward
> withdrew the application, Mrs. Hostetter laughed,
> said it was all very embarrassing, and she might
> have something to tell later.

The next day, the newspaper was able to report that the businessman and the widow had spent the evening in each other's company
but that the former had left for Berlin the next day. A few days later,
the paper informed its readers that despite the rumors, the engagement
hadn't been broken off.

In early December, Anson returned from Germany and married the
widow—although not in Saint George's church in Mayfair, which he'd
initially supplied as the location, but at a registry office, with a blessing
afterward in a small parish church on Onslow Square. Only then was it
clear what had caused the problem: the minister at Saint George's had
refused to execute the marriage because Allene wasn't formally a widow,
but a divorcée.

The necessarily modest character of the ceremony didn't prevent the bride from celebrating her third wedding in style: her wedding dress was cut from virginal white velvet and lined with white sable. Greta, as bridesmaid, was dressed in white, too. Aside from Anson's sister and his colleague Edward Rice, only Allene's friend Lady Olive Greville and her husband, along with Greta's friend Mary and her mother, attended. After the service, the small company lunched at Claridge's and the newly married couple left for a honeymoon in Monte Carlo and Nice, where Allene could introduce her parents to her new partner in life.

Clearly Greta didn't feel like visiting her maternal grandparents, who were so absent from her life that days after her coming-out the *New York Times* had mentioned "the late Charles H. Tew." A few days after the wedding, she took a boat back home to spend Christmas and New Year's with her younger brother. Anson and Allene rang in the New Year—1913—and their new life in the Ritz Hotel in London.

***

Looking back, that year with the unlucky number in it might be considered one of the best in the history of the world. The twentieth century was still young and promising. Never before had citizens of the world been able to travel and communicate so easily with one another; never before had permanent world peace seemed so attainable. There was political stability, there was prosperity, and, perhaps most important, there was a widespread optimism that everything would become even better. Bloody wars and devastating famines seemed things of a barbarian past, banished for good by the achievements of modern times. It was, in the words of writer Stefan Zweig, "the golden age of security."

In New York, the Woolworth Building, the tallest building in the world at an impressive fifty-six stories, was completed. It was designed by Cass Gilbert, who had built Allene's elegant house on East Sixty-Fourth Street. That same year, New York Harbor surpassed London's as the busiest in the world. And as always, the almost thirty-year-old Statue of Liberty beckoned to immigrants, who were still arriving by the thousands in the land of unprecedented opportunities: "Come to me, to the best country in the world, where everyone, regardless of their past, background, or gender, has the chance to make something of their life."

More than ever, this was genuinely the case. In 1913, the United States was one of the first countries to introduce income tax and to start building up a welfare system. The enormous differences in income were reduced, and capital was generated to lay roads and build schools, hospitals, libraries, and other institutions that would benefit every American citizen, rich or poor.

For Allene, 1913 was mainly a year of unprecedented happiness. An end had come to her restless travels across the world's oceans, to the endless series of parties and dinners with bored European aristocrats, and to the need for her constant efforts to clamber her way up the social ladder. An end had also come to difficult marriages and their accompanying dramas and loneliness. She had finally found a stable companion in this calm engineer, so different from her in character but so similar in background. "He was the one," as a niece of hers would later say.

It didn't matter that Allene's figure wasn't as girlishly slender as before; she'd said farewell to the latest fashions. In New York, she barely showed herself, and she disappeared from the society columns almost entirely. Anson sold his house on Madison Avenue and gave Allene's house on East Sixty-Fourth Street as his New York address from then on. But the center of their life was on Long Island, in a house that Anson had had built some years before beside a dirt track near the village of Lattingtown.

***

Long Island, the 120-mile-long peninsula east of Manhattan with the ocean lapping at both its sides, had counted as New York's Gold Coast for as long as human memory could recall. More than half of America's richest families had a country or beach house there. The writer F. Scott Fitzgerald, who set his famous novel *The Great Gatsby* there, described it as "the old island here that flowered once for Dutch sailors' eyes—a fresh, green breast of the new world."

With the completion of a rail link and, in particular, the Queensboro Bridge in 1909, the journey time between the peninsula and Manhattan was reduced so much that "ordinary" commuting became possible. The still-rural countryside was taken over by "the wealthy aristocrats of Long Island who make their living shearing lambs on Wall Street and who want to play at the country life on weekends and holidays," in the words of one concerned local. The rich aristocrats who spent their weekdays "shearing lambs" on Wall Street mainly bought up ranches around picturesque spots like Oyster Bay and Glen Cove. There they built large country houses surrounded by landscaped gardens and parks.

Lattingtown, the village where Anson built Birchwood (the name he gave his country house), lay in the heart of Locust Valley, a still relatively unspoiled area in the center of Long Island, less than an hour by train from Manhattan. From there it was just a short drive to Matinecock, where Portledge, the country estate of Anson's boss and friend Charles Coffin (who withdrew from the daily management of General Electric in 1913), was situated. Birchwood, built in neocolonial style, had twenty-three rooms, a swimming pool, a tennis court, its own farm, and a garage for eight cars. There were no ballrooms or reception rooms—it was clearly more of a place to enjoy than to impress.

Life on "Longuyland," as the inhabitants affectionately called the peninsula, was just as relaxed and uncomplicated. People met up at the Piping Rock Club, the country club that Coffin had set up, where barbecues, dances, hunting weekends, and car rallies, as well as swimming, tennis, and sailing competitions, were organized in the summer. In the winter, when Locust Valley was covered in a thick layer of snow and the many lakes and pools froze over, people entertained themselves with skating and bobsledding. Aside from this, both Coffin and Anson were active members of the Matinecock Neighborhood Association, which liaised with the local farming community and set up all kinds of services for the common good, such as free medical clinics, a library, a fire department, and a committee that implemented measures against the plagues of mosquitoes in the summer.

Perhaps the Gilded Age mansions on the Long Island coast were replete with the hedonism F. Scott Fitzgerald immortalized in *The Great Gatsby*, but here in the countryside in 1913, there was clearly no longer any interest in the frivolities and snobbery that had colored the lives of the previous generation of the wealthy. Even "new" communities like the Italians and Jews were welcome, as the membership register of the Piping Rock Club testifies. After all the excesses of the previous decades, people longed for the simplicity and moral values of America's old pioneering society, the kind Allene and Anson had experienced in their childhoods.

6

Dogfight

Teddy Hostetter was a strange fish, the freshmen at Harvard University agreed. One of his fellow students would later write:

> Teddy was an unusual fellow . . . He had all the traits of a genius. His mind was active, alert and keen, especially so along mathematical and scientific lines. Although he had a sunny disposition, a man had to know him to see his true worth. Teddy had idiosyncrasies with which all uncommon men are possessed, and which, when found in a freshman, would not be appreciated by his classmates. Those of us who knew him valued those finer qualities which made him the unusual fellow he was.

At the Pomfret School, the expensive boarding school in New England Teddy had attended from the age of fifteen onward, both his behavior and grades had been so substandard that, in the end, he was expelled. Not that anyone considered this a serious problem—elite preparatory schools like Pomfret guaranteed their pupils automatic entrance to one of the country's Ivy League universities, however badly behaved, unintelligent, or lazy they might be. And in Teddy's case, there was no question of the latter.

Teddy had inherited his father's love of sailing and his mother's love of horseback riding. He shared a passion for technology, cars, and generally anything that moved at speed with his new stepfather, with whom he got along significantly better than he had with the previous one. Teddy was also a cheerful young man, and handsome—the spitting image of Allene, in a slightly darker version. The only thing he didn't like was being dictated to—not by teachers, not by fellow pupils, and certainly not by what people expected of him. And he didn't have much need to be, with an inheritance of more than $3 million to his name.

Although his sister, Greta, seemed much more conformist than her younger brother, when it came down to it, she had exactly the same kind of willfulness. While her mother probably wanted to turn her back on Pittsburgh for good, Greta didn't. She had been eleven at the time of her father's death and their abrupt departure for New York—old enough to remember her happy father and the good times in her parents' marriage and old enough, too, to feel a permanent part of the Hostetter clan.

In particular, she was extremely close to her uncle Herbert and his family of five children, who had moved to New York. At her request, her uncle even bought back the Hostetter House on Raccoon Creek, which had been sold in 1905, seven years later so she would have her own place in the Pittsburgh vicinity, where she could easily remain in contact with the rest of her father's family. It was probably not very surprising that after being dragged halfway across the globe by her mother in search of a husband for her, Greta found one, in the end, in the smoky industrial city on three rivers and, in the early spring of 1914, brought home a Pittsburgher.

***

It is hard to imagine that Allene and Anson would have been genuinely happy with Greta's choice. Glenn Stewart was the only son and heir of self-made millionaire David Stewart, who had begun his career as a clerk and built up one of the largest grain empires. The towering Glenn was known to be fairly eccentric at a young age. During his studies at Yale, he'd crafted his own explosive to frighten a couple of girls who had opted to go to a friend's party instead of his. The bomb prematurely exploded in his face, costing him his left eye and scarring half of his face. Since then, he'd worn a monocle in front of his glass eye and adorned himself with a golden cigarette holder and a moustache so thin it almost seemed penciled on his face.

In the six years since Glenn had left the university, nothing had come of his plans to enter the diplomatic service. He didn't show any interest in the family business, either; his father simply sold the business in 1919, in the absence of a successor. Instead, Glenn traveled around the world in a spendthrift, unconventional manner. As a newspaper would write: "He was embarking on a globe-trotting and, by all accounts, eccentric and luxurious life." By the time he met Greta—in February 1914 at the wedding of one of her cousins in Allegheny—he was already in his thirties and in possession of a serious reputation. He was, as a family member once succinctly put it, "a liar, a womanizer, and a no-account."

A liar, a womanizer, and a no-account—not exactly the kind of man Allene and Anson would have wanted to entrust their naive daughter and stepdaughter to. But what were the alternatives? Greta was already well into her twenties and had little more to occupy her time than some charity work. She devoted herself to New York children who had become invalids when they suffered from tuberculosis and trained as a social worker at the New York School of Philanthropy. She dreamed of having children of her own, so no one would have wished the life of a bluestocking spinster—as single women were seen in those times—upon her.

And so on May 10, 1914, Mr. and Mrs. Burchard announced their daughter's engagement to Mr. Glenn Stewart in the *New York Times*. The couple, the paper wrote, would leave after the wedding for the Cuban capital, Havana, where Glenn had been given a post as second secretary at the American embassy. The appointment was undoubtedly due to an intervention by his future father-in-law, who as a high-ranking figure at one of the largest companies in the United States had excellent connections with the government in Washington.

Anson, who adored his two stepchildren, also tried to give the forthcoming marriage the best possible start. As a wedding present he gave Greta Birchwood's accompanying farm and had a brand-new stable built for her horses. Whatever the future might bring, she'd always have her own house close to her mother and him.

Allene, in turn, gave her daughter the grand wedding she'd never had herself. In the early morning of October 21, 1914, a special train brought more than three hundred guests from New York's Pennsylvania Station to Lattingtown. The Hostetters, as well as family and friends of Glenn's, turned out in great numbers: almost all of the twelve bridesmaids and page boys were from Pittsburgh.

The ceremony itself took place in the Lattingtown Union Chapel, a small church that had been financed almost entirely by members of the Piping Rock Club. The marriage was consecrated by one of Glenn's cousins; another cousin was best man. Allene had copiously decorated the train, the chapel, and Birchwood, where the wedding breakfast and the reception took place, with autumn leaves and gold- and copper-colored chrysanthemums. It turned the event into "a Chrysanthemum Wedding" as the *New York Times* captioned it.

Greta's wedding dress and her bridesmaids' outfits were deemed worthy of a separate article in the paper because they had been designed by an American talent at a time when Europe was still considered leading in terms of fashion and taste. The honeymoon was also an all-American affair. After a visit to Pittsburgh, the newlyweds went on to Mount Mitchell, the highest of the Blue Ridge Mountains in the Appalachians, where they went trekking and mule packing.

Meanwhile, there was nothing in the society sections about the real reason for the patriotic nature of their wedding in Lattingtown. The reader would have to turn to the front pages, which were growing considerably gloomier in tone, for that. Those who had seen in the sinking of the *Titanic* more than two years earlier a foreboding of more shocking events to come were right. Something that had seemed to Americans impossible in this new century, something they had not been expecting and did not want, had nevertheless occurred: a major war had broken out in Europe.

***

The direct cause of the conflict, everyone agreed, was the murder of the heir to the Austro-Hungarian throne, Franz Ferdinand, in Sarajevo on June 28, 1914. "Heir to Austria's Throne Slain with His Wife by a Bosnian Youth to Avenge Seizure of His Country" said the *New York Times*. Opinions weren't divided about the political background to this, either. It had mainly to do with the German Empire, created in 1871 under the leadership of Chancellor Otto von Bismarck, which was keen to see its growing economic power translated into international political influence. But how it was possible for the war to spread across Europe so quickly after the incident in Sarajevo, setting the world on fire almost immediately, was a matter that historians would puzzle over for a long time to come.

The fact was the Europeans who marched to war late that summer were literally singing and had decorated their guns with flowers. Possessed by a kind of romantic war heroism that really belonged to the previous century, they were convinced that they would soon return home triumphant. But what was then modern technology turned out to have fundamentally transformed the practice of warfare. By that fall, armies were stuck in trench lines that ran from northern France to deep in Europe. From the trenches, the warring parties hit each other with ever-heavier ammunition—sacrificing lives day after day, with no one able to break through.

Czarist Russia sided with France and England; Austria-Hungary and the Ottoman Empire fought on the German side, assisted after a while by Bulgaria. America anxiously stayed on the sidelines. Weren't these kinds of idiotic wars, instigated by megalomaniac aristocrats and parading soldiers, one of the main reasons so many immigrants had left everything behind to seek out the peace and prosperity of the New World?

It wasn't until the passenger ship RMS *Lusitania* was torpedoed by German submarines on May 7, 1915, taking down with it 128 American citizens, including millionaire's son Alfred Vanderbilt, that the United States bared its teeth. The German generals, who realized all too well that they wouldn't stand a chance in hell if mighty America sided with the Allies, hastily backed down: the submarine war would remain limited and the safety of American vessels would be assured. With this, America could comfortably resume its neutral position. The country was by then making money from the war, which, despite triumphant bulletins from both sides, never seemed headed for an end.

Month after month, the conflict oscillated around a front line that ran across Europe like a suppurating wound, feeding itself with young lives. There were days, as in July 1916 at the Somme, during which 60,000 young soldiers died for what in retrospect turned out to be a couple hundred yards of territorial gain. Or the ten-month-long "Hell of Verdun" that, when it ended in December 1916, was ultimately responsible for an incredible death toll of more than 700,000 lives.

Parents lost sons and women their fiancés; countries their young men, their prosperity, and their future. The entire international community looked to America: when would the most powerful nation in

the New World finally accept her moral responsibility and put an end
to the pointless butchery on the Continent?

***

Somewhere in the fall of 1916, Anson and his friends began to discuss in
muted tones, after dinner and with their cigars and port, the possibility
that American neutrality might not be sustainable. An international
concern like General Electric that also operated in Europe received
war updates on a daily basis. They knew, for example, that great dissatisfaction with the czarist regime was brewing among the Russian
population. The February revolution and the subsequent collapse of
the Russian side on the east front indeed gave the Germans a welcome
respite; they could now concentrate their efforts on the Western Front.
Determined to force a breakthrough, the high command called for a
total submarine war.

Now America no longer had a choice. On April 6, 1917, President
Woodrow Wilson, who a few months earlier had won an election by
promising not to take part in the conflict, declared war on Germany.
Six days later, Anson and Allene, together on the *Empress of Russia*, left
from Vancouver, Canada, for China and Japan, for what was officially
termed a three-month business trip.

Both the timing—precisely when international travel was more
dangerous than ever—and the destination suggest that Anson was,
in fact, on a reconnaissance mission for the American government.
China had up to that point shown itself a solid partner to the Allies,
but the traditionally anti-British Japanese empire was all too happy to
be courted by the Germans. Later, the ambassador Anson and Allene
stayed with in Tokyo would write in his memoirs that the atmosphere
in Japan with regard to America "could be cut with a knife."

At the end of July, Anson and Allene returned home, again via
Canada, and found their country in an early, excited, and almost

infatuated stage of war. The arms factories were running at full speed, and there were improvised encampments everywhere in which volunteers stood at the ready for the journey to France. The first American regiments had already landed in Europe on June 26, 1917, bursting with impatience to show the world what American heroism looked like.

Across the country, posters of Uncle Sam urged recruits to sign up: "I want YOU!"—and almost the entire Burchard family complied. Anson was drafted by the War Department in Washington to work for Assistant Secretary of War Benedict Crowell. Allene and a few friends from Locust Valley set up a committee to raise money for Hospitality House in New York, a place for young officers on leave. The mother of Kitty Kimball, Teddy's girlfriend, left for France to work as a nurse. Teddy himself signed up on August 19 as an aspiring pilot in the British air force, the Royal Flying Corps.

***

In the eight years that had gone by since Teddy had seen an airplane circle the Statue of Liberty for the first time from his father's yacht, aviation had progressed at a great pace. If there was anything the protracted trench fighting in Europe had made clear to the governments concerned, it was that the future of modern warfare was not to be found down in the mud but up in the sky. Both the Germans and the Brits now had air fleets at their disposal containing a few thousand single-seater planes from which pilots could fire at each other with primitive machine guns far above the lines.

These sky fighters were the only ones in the world war who still radiated a certain glamour and heroism. The outcomes of the dogfights, man-against-man battles in the air, were decided by the individual courage and skill of the pilots—elements that barely counted in the mechanized massacres on the ground. What's more, the parties treated each other with a kind of old-fashioned chivalry, such as dropping messages about deaths and captures on the opponent's air bases. Flying aces like the audacious "Red Baron" Manfred von Richthofen, who managed to down as many as sixty planes, were treated as heroes by both friends and enemies.

In the fall of 1917, since America didn't yet have its own air force in the war, thousands of young Americans signed up for the Royal Flying Corps. Most of them were young men like Teddy from rich upper-class families, fascinated by danger and speed, bored to death by the life their parents had set up for them and their fake studies at Ivy League universities—young men who spotted an opportunity to actually mean something by joining the war in the sky.

"The RFC attracted adventurous spirits, devil-may-care youth, fast livers, furious drivers and risk-takers, who invested the Corps with a certain style and mystique," wrote pilot and writer Cecil Lewis in his aviation classic *Sagittarius Rising*. The admissions requirements were simple: the candidate should be a sporty—a euphemism for over-confident—type and be able to ride horses and drive a car. Rich, in other words, since these were expensive hobbies the average American couldn't afford.

Teddy Hostetter was the perfect candidate. And now that he had finally found something he really felt passionate about, he became a model student for the first time in his life. He completed his training at record speed. The first part took place in the United States and consisted of six weeks of general military training followed by his first real flight training. For most of the cadets, flying overshadowed everything else. In the words of one of Teddy's fellow students:

> It's a great life, mother, flying alone with nothing to worry about, the whole sky to fly in and not much work to do. I will really hate to see this old war stop, if it ever does. I am having such a fine time!

The second part of the training, the actual training to be a fighter pilot, took place in England. Teddy was just able to celebrate Christmas 1917 at Birchwood, where he wrote a will leaving everything to his mother and sister in equal parts. He also took the opportunity to get engaged to his girlfriend, Kitty. On January 6, 1918, he saw the three most important women in his life grow smaller and smaller on the shores of New York as he sailed away from his homeland, past the Statue of Liberty, on his way to a war he had made his mission.

***

Teddy, the "strange fish" at Harvard, turned out to be a born aviator. He was promoted to second lieutenant after just one month and moved to the RFC's No. 67 Training Squadron. At the No. 2 (Auxiliary) School of Aerial Gunnery, on the southwestern coast of Scotland, he learned to use a machine gun and drop bombs from an aircraft onto a target on the ground. In the early morning of April 3, 1918, he left for France to join the No. 54 Squadron of what was by then called the Royal Air Force, stationed in Calais. That very same day he made his maiden combat flight.

The 54 Squadron had originally been set up as an escort for bombing raids, but since the Battle of Arras in 1917, it had specialized in so-called low-level attack missions, in which enemy observation balloons were eliminated with bombs and machine-gun fire. It meant the pilots flew low to the ground, diving within range of enemy artillery. The squadron flew Sopwith Camels, which weren't just the most advanced aircraft in the British air force but also the most dangerous. The engine's cooling system caused a strong torque to the right during flight, which made takeoff and landing a risky business. Aside from this, minor damage to the planes, which were built from oilcloth and wood, could result in a burning inferno within seconds. The pilots weren't given parachutes; these were considered unsporting and could also have led to unnecessary loss of machinery. The average life expectancy of a fighter pilot was no more than fifty to sixty flight hours. This came to about four weeks, depending on the weather conditions.

It looked like Teddy's war was going to be even shorter. Late in the day on April 11, eight days after his first flight above the battle lines, he was hit by German machine-gun fire from the ground. Although his legs were seriously injured, he managed to land his plane safely on the Allied side of the line. After having his wounds treated at a hospital in the coastal town of Wimereux, he was transported back to England to recover further. In late May, he was released from the hospital to recover at No. 7 Aircraft Acceptance Park, a former golf course near London where airplanes were assembled in large hangars.

At that moment, the chances didn't seem great that Teddy would ever return to the war, undoubtedly to the great relief and hope of the women he'd left behind on the shores of New York. In June 1918, a major German offensive led to nothing. The Allies now finally seemed to hold the winning hand, partly thanks to a weapon developed in America that seemed to supply a long-awaited solution to trench warfare: the tank. Although in the *Vaterland*, which was exhausted and depleted after four years of war, German Kaiser Wilhelm II continued to make warmongering speeches, it now seemed only a matter of time before his generals would come to their senses and finally end their losing battle.

Against all expectations, however, the complete collapse of the German front failed to occur. The Germans had dug themselves into the as-good-as-impregnable Hindenburg Line and seemed keener to fight to the death than to surrender. And Teddy, who had been champing at the bit all summer because there was nothing he wanted more than to be able to fly and fight, managed to get approval for a return to active duty in early August. On August 16, 1918, he reported to the central assembly point for all troops leaving for the Continent, and on

September 5, he crossed the English Channel for the second time, once again as a fighter pilot headed to France.

***

For a short while, Teddy was put to work at a supply depot in Marquise—this was probably at the request of Anson Burchard, who did everything he could behind the scenes in Washington to keep his impetuous stepson out of the danger zone at the tail end of the war. But on September 18, no more excuses could be found to keep Teddy on the ground any longer, and he was allowed to report to the No. 3 Squadron, which was under command of the famous flying ace Major Ronald McClintock. He went back up into the sky that very evening.

Nine days later, September 27, 1918—Greta celebrated her twenty-seventh birthday that day—began what promised to be one of the last, if not the very last, battles of the world war. The target was a number of large underground tunnels along the Canal du Nord near Cambrai, reputed to be one of the toughest parts of the Hindenburg Line to crack.

At seven o'clock that evening, Teddy and four other pilots were instructed to destroy a few German observation balloons above the Canal de l'Escaut, between the locks of Masnières and Saint-Vaast. After a half hour of flying, a German aircraft appeared in their sights, and they managed to shoot it down. Teddy and a fellow pilot dived down to finish the job with bombs. At that moment, several German planes appeared and attacked the patrol from above. After a short but intense dogfight, the three British planes at the highest altitude were able to evade the enemy attack and return their planes safely to base. The two other planes failed to return home that evening.

Two days later, Masnières was taken by ground troops. No trace was found of the two missing pilots or their planes. Another two days later, a telegram from the British Air Ministry arrived at Birchwood:

"Lieutenant Hostetter was reported missing on September 27, having failed to return from flying duty." A few days later, a letter followed in which Teddy's commanding officer provided the family with more details surrounding the young pilot's disappearance and the impression he'd left during the short time he'd been under his command:

> Your son came to the squadron on the 18th of September, and though he was only a short time with us, showed great keenness for his work and was rapidly becoming a fine pilot whom we could afford ill to lose. He was extremely popular among us and we all feel his absence very keenly. I wish you the sincere sympathy of all members of the squadron for the great anxiety you must feel.

***

The letter from Teddy's commander reached Allene and Anson at a moment when America was in the grip of a major panic. In late August, a mysterious illness, which had first appeared that summer in southern Europe and was therefore called the "Spanish flu," had taken its first victims in Boston. From one moment to the next, perfectly healthy people developed coughs, high fevers, sore throats, and severe muscle pain. Sometimes they died within the space of a few hours, sometimes within a few days, literally drowning in the liquid of their infected lungs as their skin turned a bluish black from a lack of oxygen.

Since then, the illness had spread across almost the entire continent at an alarming rate. While over a four-year period more than sixteen million people died in the First World War, Spanish flu managed to claim fifty million victims worldwide in just half a year. It was as though nature wanted to mimic the mass murder that humans had perpetrated upon themselves. A quarter of the American population fell sick. In hastily erected encampments on the edges of cities, doctors could do no more than just watch their patients die, often without even having the time to take their temperature. Surprisingly enough, those who were the most vulnerable during regular flu epidemics, such as children and old people, had the best chance of survival. The illness hit hardest young, healthy adults with strong immune systems, such as Teddy's sister, Greta.

Until this, Greta had experienced a safe war, first in Cuba and then in Guatemala and Vienna, where her husband was stationed at embassies. After America declared war, the couple returned home and Glenn was given an insignificant post in Washington. Greta had become pregnant in 1917 but had miscarried. She'd buried her stillborn child a stone's throw from her family home in Locust Valley, in the pretty cemetery at the end of Feeks Lane that the area's rich inhabitants had had designed a few years earlier by a son of Central Park architect Frederick Law Olmsted. Now she was pregnant again and, to her great joy, with twins.

But sometime in the early weeks of October, as the entire Burchard family was on tenterhooks awaiting news about Teddy, a gray shadow also slipped into Greta's house in Washington and laid a chilly hand on her shoulder. Shortly afterward, she began to cough. She died on Wednesday, October 16. The twin brothers who would have been Allene and Anson's first grandchildren didn't survive.

On Friday, October 18, Allene bade farewell to her daughter. The funeral took place in the same chapel in Lattingtown where Greta, in her American bridal gown, had married Glenn almost four years previously to the day. Later that afternoon she was buried next to the place she'd earlier chosen for her stillborn baby.

That same evening, the wheels of an army jeep crunched over the gravel drive of a Birchwood already immersed in grief. There was news about Teddy. Inhabitants of Masnières had reported seeing an airplane crash on the evening of September 27 on the Chemin des Rues des Vignes, outside the village. The Germans had removed the airplane, but the pilot had been buried in a shallow grave at the site, still wearing his lieutenant's uniform. Now his identity had been determined with certainty.

Later one of Teddy's fellow pilots would write a melancholy poem about their war experiences, despairing that it had all been for nothing:

> We flew together, in the tall blue sky
> We fought together, with bombs and guns
> We ate together, in the squadron mess
> We danced together, to the old gramophone
>
> We walked together, in the fields of France
> We talked together, of home and tomorrow
> We flew together in the tall blue sky
> Many were killed. The world is no better.

Teddy, too, had flown in the tall blue sky and fought with guns and bombs. He, too, had eaten in the squadron mess and danced with his comrades to the sounds of an old gramophone; he had walked through French fields, talking about the future. But for him it was now certain that no "home and tomorrow" would come.

7

The Crippled Heart

In her later lives, after she'd changed her name, continent, hair color, and even her year of birth, Allene would almost never speak of her children, and not even of Anson. Only in passing: "Yesterday we were at Teddy's grave. There were flowers there and so peaceful." Or, "Anson always used to say if one was busy they did not seem to mind the heat too much." But holding forth on sorrow or grief, on the dreams she'd had for Greta and Teddy, was not something Allene did. Indeed, most of the people she socialized with in her later years didn't even know she'd once had children.

Clearly a child of the nineteenth century, Allene hadn't yet been infected with the modern idea that grief was a thing that needed to be processed or could even be healed, preferably by talking a lot. For the Victorians, fate was simply something to be borne, and that is what she did, without complaining. Her situation was like that of many others who were left behind like street litter after the world war. Just as they had to find a way to get through life with their missing limbs, blasted-away faces, and fractured nerves, so did she with her crippled heart.

On November 11, 1918, the warring parties signed an armistice in the French Compiègne, and the war was finally over. Teddy Hostetter's death was old news by then. Harvard's secretarial office collected in a slender file the few newspaper clippings and bits and pieces—"Harvard graduate fails to return from air raid" and "sad but proud duty"—with which the Pomfret School had marked the death of its former pupil. Afterward the file labeled "T. R. Hostetter" disappeared into their archives with the accompanying note: "Death card made."

At the end of November, when the Spanish flu had burned itself out just as unexpectedly as it had flared up and people cautiously dared to socialize again, a memorial service for Lieutenant Hostetter was held in Saint Bartholomew's Church on Park Avenue. There was no coffin. Immediately after they were recovered, Teddy's remains had been reburied at one of the improvised burial grounds established in France in those days. But Allene kept the four flags used during the service— the Stars and Stripes, the Royal Air Force's banner, and those of the 54 and 3 Squadrons—flying for weeks afterward at the Hospitality House for Junior Officers she had helped set up on Lexington Avenue, where young officers who had returned from France cheerfully went about their business.

In Lattingtown, a memorial plaque was placed on the town library with the names of the 132 young men from the community who had fought in Europe. There was a gold star after three of those names, Teddy's included, to indicate that they had paid with their lives. Greta and her children were memorialized, too. Just as Allene had ornamented the glory days of her daughter's youth with flowers—wild roses for her graduation ceremony, spring flowers for her coming-out, and golden chrysanthemums for her wedding—she did the same for Greta's death. A simple stone cross the height of a man, bearing Greta's name surrounded by numerous decorative entwined lilies carved out of the hard stone, was placed on her grave.

Then it was Christmas in an empty, quiet Birchwood, where memories of the past, when they were all together, were almost palpable in the rooms. And a new year dawned with nothing positive to offer. No joyous births, no wedding of Teddy and Kitty. No plans, no hope. No becoming a grandmother, no longer being a mother.

Of course, other families in the United States were painfully confronted with empty places at the dinner table during the holidays—in total more than eighteen thousand young Americans had died. But it seemed that nowhere had fate so cruelly and definitively lashed out as on Allene's happy island, which shortly before had appeared so safe.

***

On February 17, 1919, the biggest and most triumphant victory parade that New York had ever seen moved along Fifth Avenue. Among more than a million spectators cheering on the returning soldiers was a young F. Scott Fitzgerald, who would later describe the memorable day in an essay in *My Lost City*:

> New York had all the iridescence of the beginning of the world. The returning troops marched up Fifth Avenue and girls were instinctively drawn east and north towards them—this was the greatest nation and there was gala in the air [. . .] We felt like small children in a great bright unexplored barn.

While New York was ringing in the world's new start by drinking, dancing, and making love, about fifty miles away Allene was mourning the end of her world in the wintery silence of Locust Valley. A few days after the parade, Anson could take it no more and applied for new passports for the both of them; their previous ones had been taken away in connection with travel restrictions imposed during the submarine hostilities.

Since international travel was still limited, Anson had to prove that the journey he wanted to make was of crucial importance. His boss, the CEO of General Electric, argued in a letter that after four and a half years of war, it was essential that one of his staff go and assess the status of the company's European interests in person and that they'd invited Mr. Burchard to do this. A comparable document was prepared for Allene, with a personal note from Anson's boss:

> It affords me pleasure to testify to the high character, loy-
> alty and patriotism of Mrs. Burchard. She has been active
> in the connections with important relief work during the
> war period, and is in all respects qualified for the issuance
> of a passport.

On the photograph attached to the passport application, Allene is looking straight into the camera—still a handsome woman at forty-six years old. But there is something in her gaze that makes the spectator almost uncomfortable. Anson, in his passport photo, mainly looks concerned and very, very serious.

The application was granted, and on April 12, 1919, the Burchards boarded the RMS *Aquitania* for Liverpool. From there they traveled to Paris, where at least they were able to take Teddy's fiancée in their arms again. The daughter of a famous New York book publisher, Kitty Kimball had spent most of her childhood in the French capital and had decided earlier that winter to travel to the continent that had robbed her of her future husband. She now worked as a correspondent for the American glossy magazine *Victory*, in which she had a column titled "Notes of an American in France."

By then, Kitty had been able to gather more information about Teddy's last flight. He had been shot down by Robert Greim, a colleague of the famous Red Baron. This experienced fighter pilot had gone hunting for his twenty-fifth airborne victory that fateful day in September; his exploits would earn him a military medal and a knighthood. The young New Yorker hadn't stood the slightest chance against him. At the end of the air battle, Greim had landed to take pictures of his crashed opponent. He'd added the photographs to his logbook as proof.

Masnières, the village above which Teddy had fought his last dog-fight, turned out to be an unremarkable farming hamlet on the Canal de l'Escaut of which only a collection of ruins was left after four years in the heat of battle. Allene and Anson decided on the spot to donate 100,000 francs to the community for the construction of a boys' school that would carry the name of their late son. Not that their son had been such an enthusiastic school attendee, but his parents were still Victorian enough to be convinced of the value of good schooling for all.

***

The Burchards traveled across the afflicted continent for six months. They visited Allene's parents, who had been able to continue their quiet life in Nice virtually undisturbed by the war. They visited Italy, which had suffered terribly during the conflict; they passed through countries that had remained neutral and were untouched, like Spain, Switzerland, and the Netherlands; and they went to Belgium, where the traces of destruction were omnipresent. In late October 1919, they returned home from Cherbourg, France, on the SS *Lapland*, just in time to attend the ceremony at which Harvard was granting Teddy a posthumous bachelor of science for his "honorable war service."

Once home, Allene bought a country house with a large plot of land and its own little harbor in Roslyn, a coastal village not far from Lattingtown. She had it refurbished as a holiday resort and put the Greta-Theo Holiday House, as she named it, at the disposal of a New York association for single working young women. Over the following summers, she would be a familiar sight at the wheel of a truck filled to the brim with live chickens or cabbages and other vegetables from the farm at Birchwood, all intended for her protégées.

Greta's widower, Glenn Stewart, had found his own way of picking up the pieces of his life. In November 1919, barely a year after the death of his first wife, he quietly married Cecile "Jacqueline" Archer, the daughter of a wealthy missionary and businessman from Arkansas. Over the years, Glenn had become a thorn in the side of the diplomatic service. He came and went as it suited him, and the only time he handed in anything resembling a report, its quality was so abominable that his manager complained, "This is without exception the most careless and almost illiterate document I have ever seen." Not long after his second wedding, Glenn was fired. Anson evidently saw no need to protect his son-in-law anymore.

Incidentally, this time Glenn had chosen a woman who trumped him in terms of eccentricity. Jacqueline was in the habit of dying her poodles the same colors as the interiors of her Cadillacs, and in 1926, she'd make the society pages by giving the famous film star Rudolph Valentino a 177-pound Irish wolfhound she'd bred, valued at $5,000. In the end, the wealthy couple would withdraw in increasing paranoia to a fake castle on Wye Island, on the coast of Maryland, they'd designed themselves. It was from there that one day Glenn sailed off on his yacht into the deep blue sea and was never seen again.

***

And so began a new decade as the Roaring Twenties burst out in all their vitality. In New York both skyscrapers and skirts reached new heights. Flappers—as fashionable young women would become known—cast overboard the corsets, long skirts, long hair, and social and sexual conventions of their Victorian predecessors. They went to jazz clubs to dance the Lindy Hop in honor of Charles Lindbergh, the first pilot who managed to fly across the Atlantic Ocean.

Twentieth-century consumerism spread to the farthest corners of America, and luxury goods that up to the First World War had been reserved for the very rich, like cars and refrigerators, were now within reach of the great masses. For $290 you could buy yourself a Ford Model T. Industry and prosperity grew, and New York definitively replaced London as the world's financial center. America was now, indeed and indisputably, the greatest nation.

These were busy years for Anson. In 1922, he was appointed vice chairman of the board of directors and CEO of the international branch of still-expanding General Electric. Aside from this, he had dozens of ancillary and volunteer roles in organizations, including the Automobile Club of America and the New York Chamber of Commerce and Industry, where he was chairman of the selection committee. Allene, too, kept herself busy. If she wasn't accompanying her husband on one of his many business trips to Europe, she was active on the charity circuit, raising money in particular for veterans' organizations and hospitals. She also made her name as an art collector; in 1921, she became a sustaining member of the Metropolitan Museum of Art. That same year, she made a comeback to the society columns from which she'd been practically absent for more than three years.

Just as disabled war veterans were being fitted for artificial limbs or having masks painted to cover their mutilated faces, Allene seemed to be filling the hole in her heart with surrogate children—young people to whom she could offer the love she could no longer give Greta and Teddy. She became a kind of replacement mother for Jane Moinson, a young woman she and Anson had met in France in the summer of 1919. The only daughter of Paris surgeon Louis Moinson, Jane had just lost her own mother and could do with some care and diversion.

In May 1921, after two consecutive winters with the Burchards, Jane was presented to the New York social scene, marking her coming-out as a debutante with a whole series of lunches, dinners, and even a ball organized by her hostess. Soon a suitable marriage candidate for the young Parisienne announced himself in the form of Cyrus W. Miller, a young engineer from General Electric. They married in June at a large wedding at Birchwood attended by more than three hundred guests.

A year later it was the turn of another "daughter" of Allene and Anson. Kitty, who'd returned to the United States, had found new love in the person of banker and war veteran Henry Wallace Cohu. Wally, as everyone called him, had been one of the groomsmen at Jane Moinson's wedding. They married in the summer of 1922 at Kitty's parents' house on Long Island. With the financial backing of the Burchards, who acted as silent partners in his firm, Wally then set up his own investment bank.

And then there was the family of Allene's cousin Julia Warner, the daughter of one of Allene's father's sisters. She and Allene were only a couple of years apart in age and practically grew up together in Jamestown. Later, Julia married Charles Rosewater, the son of newspaper owner Edward Rosewater, who after a number of setbacks in business had decided to settle with his family in New York.

The Burchards were particularly fond of the Rosewaters, and, curiously, their friends' children were strikingly similar to the ones they had lost themselves. Julia's elder child, Charlotte, was by a twist of nature the spitting image of Greta—the two could have been sisters. And her younger, Seth, was just as interested in engineering as Teddy had been and was determined to start work as an engineer at General Electric like his uncle Anson.

***

As she and Anson assembled a replacement family around them, Allene's own family crumbled. In January 1923, her mother died, followed two years later by her father. In both cases, their daughter traveled to the

South of France to take care of them for the last few months of their lives. Jennette and Charles Tew were buried in La Caucade, the old Nice graveyard high in the hills, in the area reserved for English people, so far from the village near Lake Chautauqua they'd come from.

Following the deaths of Allene's parents, she and Anson made a new start. They sold the Allene Tew Nichols House on Sixty-Fourth Street, which was weighed down with memories, and bought instead an even larger and more exclusive building on Park Avenue, which in those years had definitively taken over from Fifth Avenue as the most desirable address in America. "If America has a heaven, this is it," in the words of the liberal weekly magazine the *New Republic* in 1927.

The new house, which took over the entire southwestern corner of Park Avenue and Sixty-Ninth Street, had been commissioned eight years earlier by banker Henry Pomeroy Davison, who had a country house in Lattingtown and was well known by the Burchards. The new house had five floors, ten master bedrooms, fourteen servants' bedrooms, two elevators, and a built-in garage. After Davison's death in 1922, his wife put the house on the market for more than half a million dollars—an amount almost impossible to drum up in those times.

But money was not an object for the Burchards. Anson was a "genius in financial matters," according to accounts from General Electric employees, and during his long career, he had accumulated assets to the tune of several million dollars. Allene, who also had her share of financial talent, was, in the words of one of Anson's colleagues, "extremely wealthy." In addition to the fortune she had earned in the years after her divorce from her second husband, she also had the Hostetter millions at her disposal. They had been held back when her children were alive, but now she had inherited them in turn.

Almost at the time they bought the house on Park Avenue, they also bought a house in Paris, which had been very attractive to cosmopolitan, artistic, liberal Americans since the Belle Époque. Although it had been significantly impoverished by the war, the French capital had lost none of its allure and charm. And for Americans, the French dream had become only more accessible. Using riches gained in their own country, they bought up on a large scale the châteaus and city mansions the chic French families could no longer afford to keep. Around the time the Burchards bought their mansion in the eighth arrondissement, forty thousand of their fellow countrymen were registered at Paris addresses.

Allene may not have been in control of fate, but she was in control of the decoration and furnishing of her houses, and she gave this her total dedication. She decorated the large house on Park Avenue from basement to garret in French style, with wall tapestries from Versailles, among other things. Anson's large collection of English mezzotint engravings was given a place, as was the art collection they'd built up together over the years and of which a 1778 landscape by British painter Thomas Gainsborough was the undisputed high point. The result was what one of the Burchards' many friends later described with much admiration in diplomatic and business circles as "a delightful house."

With their alternative family as well as new domiciles on both sides of the ocean, Allene and Anson seemed to have succeeded in making a new happy island for themselves—very different from their former one but in every way livable. They were now a more than wealthy middle-aged couple with many interests and an exciting lifestyle. True, they weren't surrounded by their own children, but they did have the many friends they'd made through the years, both in America and abroad. And they had each other. In the fourteen years since their small wedding on Onslow Square, they'd been through the worst imaginable and survived it together; they could certainly brave old age and illness.

***

It was just a regular Sunday in the cold month of January 1927, and Anson, who was in his early sixties by now, did something very much in keeping with his habits: he went to have lunch with a good friend of his, the Jewish banker Mortimer Schiff, who lived a little farther along Park Avenue and, like the Burchards, had once had a country house in Locust Valley. But for Allene, the day became a living nightmare when, later that afternoon, her friends came to tell her that Anson would never, ever return home again.

The next day, newspapers reported that the top-ranking GE employee had become unwell halfway through lunch and been carried by his table companions to Schiff's library. There, on the floor, the big man had simply died, without the hurriedly called doctor being able to do anything for him. The official cause of death was "acute indigestion." In fact, it was probably a heart attack as a result of his largely sedentary lifestyle, too much work, and being overweight.

Three days later, Anson lay in state among his mezzotints in the large hall in his house on Park Avenue. The memorial service began at eleven in the morning on January 25. For the first time in its history, General Electric closed all of its offices at one o'clock in tribute to the man who had played an important role in building up the company. Anson was extremely popular among his friends and colleagues, and there was enormous sadness at his passing.

That afternoon, Allene buried the man who was her great love in the cemetery at the end of Feeks Lane in Lattingtown—close to his own Birchwood and the grave of the stepdaughter he had considered his own. After this, Allene was truly alone for the first time in years, with a heart that had been crippled for a second time. She was rich, but in terms of having people who truly belonged to her, she was poorer than even the simplest servants in her houses.

Allene was "the richest and saddest of New York's socially celebrated widows," wrote the *New York Times*, shortly after Anson's death.

***

Years later Allene would attempt to cheer up someone in her social circle. "Everyone has sadness and much trouble and likes a gay pleasant friend about," she wrote, followed in capital letters by "COURAGE ALL THE TIME." But gay and pleasant company was not something the saddest widow of New York could offer in the spring of 1927. She was no good at being a victim or dealing with pitying looks, either. The only thing she had left was courage.

At the end of the winter, the staff of the Greta-Theo Holiday House was told they would no longer have to open the house in the summer. Its owner, the explanation went, was planning to leave the country and would no longer be capable of managing it, let alone turning up with a truckload of cabbage and chickens. A hasty petition from the "Greta-Theo Girls," as Allene's holidaymakers called themselves, ensured that the entire country house would later be given to a New York charitable organization that took over the running of the resort in its founder's spirit.

On April 13, 1927, Allene set off. She traveled on the Cunard Line's flagship, the RMS *Mauretania*, on which she'd made the ocean crossing to Europe with Anson many times. Now, aged fifty-four, she was traveling alone for the first time—away from the city where too many people knew too much about her past, away from the story itself, away, too, from the memories of almost everyone she could call family. And, as the *Mauretania* plowed steadily through the lead-gray waves of this still-chilly spring month, she dropped four years from her age and left her darker hair and her past in its wake.

So many had taken the same route from Europe to America, determined to make a new start—nose to the wind, gaze focused on what lay ahead of the prow of a giant ship. Many had changed and reinvented themselves in that strange limbo between here and there on an ocean journey, preparing themselves as best they could for life on the other side. Allene did the same, but in the opposite direction, an inverse emigrant.

There were echoes of the pioneers of Allene's youth who had rebuilt, again and again, their burned-down settlement in the woods next to Lake Chautauqua and finally managed to erect an entire town. She had come from a family of strong men who had little time or patience for self-pity or weakness. What's more, she was American. And if there was one thing that was truly American, it was the belief that it was always possible to start again.

Allene, thirty-six years old, now married to Morton Nichols, portrayed in the Society section of the New York Times, *March 1909.*

MRS. MORTON C. NICHOLS,
(Mrs. Allene Tew Hostetter.)
(Photo by Anne Dupont.)

The Society section, New York Times, *1909.*

Miss Greta Hostetter's Wedding Gown and Bridesmaid's Gown of
Autumn Brown Velvet for Miss Hostetter's Wedding. Gowns by T. M.
and J. M. Fox.

Greta's wedding gown in the New York Times, *October 25, 1914.*

AMERICAN-DESIGNED DRESSES
AT MISS HOSTETTER'S WEDDING

WHEN Miss Greta Hostetter, the daughter of Mrs. Anson Burchard, was married at Locust Valley on Wednesday to Glenn Stewart, Second Secretary of the American Legation at Havana, her wedding frock, and the dresses of her attendants, offered a charming example of beautiful gowns "created" in America.

Miss Hostetter's dress was made and designed in New York. In its simplicity and dignity, in the grace of its sweeping flat-hung train, it owed nothing whatever to Paris. It is essentially an American "creation."

And the bridesmaids and maid of honor wore American "creations," too. All the gowns, the wedding dress especially, were quite girlish and simple, all fashioned with what is often thought to be a decidedly French attention to "line." But of all of them were absolutely original, very beautifully illustrative of the ability in America to make original things.

The bride's dress was a simple wedding gown, the sort of dress that a lay observer usually calls "a smart little thing" because it is both chic and girlish. The dress was complete made of cream satin, over which a draped overdress of white tulle fell in soft and graceful folds to the feet. The soft tulle bodice was caught in with a deep girdle of satin, which came up in a very sharp point over the left shoulder. On the other side a soft drapery of point lace was drawn in itself without the train, and was up from under the girdle, and formed the other side of the bodice, finishing the right shoulder.

The upper part of the bodice was cut in the new round neck line, rather low at the throat, and finished prettily with seed pearls as a smart "edging" for the tulle. Over the shoulders the tulle was drawn down to form long tight sleeves. They were slightly draped and very close fitting, but their smartest feature was the applied piece of point lace which came low over the knuckles in what can best be described as a "gauntlet" effect. Sleeves are of course very long, close, and transparent this year, and the demands of the Autumn fashion were met, in this tulle with

lace gauntlets, with a singularly graceful and original effect.

Another girlish feature of the gown was the rolled fold of cream satin heading a tulle flounce which finished the overdress and which brought added softness to the draped skirt.

The most striking single thing, however, was of course the train. The long wedding train hung from the bride's shoulders to the ground, and was fastened on each shoulder with a pretty little ornament of seed pearls. The feature of the train was its lack of fullness at the top. It was absolutely flat. It had not one ripple of fullness anywhere, and it hung perfectly straight from the shoulders to below the waist-line. There, gradually and almost unnoticeably, a little fullness began to creep in. Only a dressmaker—and an expert at that—could have told how it was done.

But imperceptibly the absolutely flat train began to ripple, more and more, until it became quite circular. At the bottom of the train there was an immense amount of cream satin fullness lying on the ground. Of course, there is more fullness at the bottom of the skirts this year than there has been for some seasons. The graceful ripple about the lower part of a skirt is "new" this year. So that this train had an uncommon amount of sheer contrast between its flat beginning at the shoulders and its circular fullness as it swept along the ground. The train was cut square at the bottom and very gracefully finished with groupings of orange blossoms on one side.

Miss Hostetter's veil, in the new circular shape, had been especially made in one piece of fine point lace, and had been ordered some time ago by the house that made her dress. It fell from her head to the edge of the long train in folds as graceful as those of the train itself.

Miss Hostetter's wedding was essentially an Autumn wedding—a chrysanthemum wedding it was called—and the attendants were dressed in Autumn colors, in gowns of interesting as well as beautiful design. The tones of the bridesmaids' dresses were Autumn brown and chrysanthemum yellow, and the bodice was cut in a smart coatee effect. This coatee was of Autumn brown velvet, and was brought down low to form a deep girdle well down over the hips and quite close-fitting. In front the bodice, which was rather plain in a general

smart effect—was fastened with bunches of brown and yellow chrysanthemums and Autumn leaves in the brown and bronze Autumn tints.

Then, in an original design, extremely frou-frou skirts of yellow tulle—a chrysanthemum tone that has the clarity of a pure corn tint—flared from the plain tailored coatee. The skirts were two, one above the other, so as to divide the sweep of the skirt almost equally in two parts. They were made over a slip of yellow satin and they were quite plain in the frou-frou fullness and very short. The low girdle which came over the top of the skirt held the tulle flat.

The entire effect was such as to prove conclusively that the striking combination of tints, materials, and even of designs, in fashions that are almost "daring" and quite fascinating, is by no means an exclusively French trait. No Parisienne could have created a more bewitching, girlish, and original design than these bridesmaid's dresses with their rich brown velvet and their flaring yellow tulle.

The sleeves were of the tulle, long and close-fitting, and the upper part of the bodice was finished with a tulle chemisette gathered at the throat with a gold cord.

The bridesmaids wore rather large picture hats of Autumn-brown velvet—the same shade as the velvet coatee—trimmed with yellow and brown chrysanthemums and Autumn leaves. And their entire costume was so arranged that the great sheaf of chrysanthemums that they carried seemed a part of the entire design.

The maid of honor wore a gown and hat made precisely like those of the bridesmaids, but with no Autumn-brown tones in the color scheme. The velvet of bodice and hat was of chrysanthemum yellow. The dresses were all, both in color and arrangement and general design, of a quite simple and quite "practicable" sort—new Autumn models created in America.

The gowns for both the bride and her attendants were made by the T. M. and J. M. Fox establishment, which has always made a specialty of wedding dresses. Mrs. Douglas, president of the company, in talking of the "creation" of gowns in America, said that the importation of ideas and clothes from France had always been more a matter of expediency than necessity.

"Owing to the tremendous pressure of work here, and the difficulty in finding time to devote exclusively to the creation of designs, as well as the inspiration of the Parisian background," she said, "we have found it for the most part easier to import our models. But there is no reason why that need be done. We are quite capable in America of creating our own designs and making our own fashions and our own clothes."

The New York Times
Published: October 25, 1914
Copyright © The New York Times

MISS GRETA HOSTETTER.

Miss Greta Hostetter in her debutante photo in the Pittsburgh Gazette.

To Wed Prince

Mrs. Anson Wood Burchard of New York, widow of the former General Electric company vice chairman, and Prince Henry XXXIII of Reuss, relative of the reigning family of Holland, will be married shortly.

Article in the Lincoln Evening Journal, *February 20, 1929.*

8

The American Princess

About a year and a half later—it was a warm August day in 1928—a forty-nine-year-old German nobleman sent a letter from Castle Stonsdorf, in the Krkonoše mountain range in Silesia in southern Germany. His name was Henry Reuss, and he was a scion of an aristocratic German family that until 1918 had counted among the oldest and most prominent in Europe. Although there was no name at the top of the letter—the recipient had to make do with the polite *"Gnädiges Fräulein"* ("My dear Miss")—its contents were intended for a governess. She had once taken care of him and his brothers and sister and now played an important role in the life of his children, who, since the death of Henry's ex-wife five years earlier, had been left semiorphaned.

Henry had, he wrote, news that was to be kept strictly confidential. It was a matter of a *"einem tief einschneidenden Ereignis"*—a life-changing event for him, but also in terms of the lives of his thirteen-year-old daughter, Marlisa, and twelve-year-old son, Heiner:

> I have got engaged and this to the widowed Mrs. Burchard, born Tew, from New York. She comes from

a strict Protestant house which is held in high regard in
America, is three years older than myself and has had three
children, all of whom she has lost [. . .] My fiancée has no
other close blood relatives and is alone in life. This is the
reason that all of her very strong motherly love, her sensitive motherly understanding and feelings go out to my
children. I know that she will become the person that both
of my darlings miss without them realizing this. And I
can already see how wonderfully their relationship is being
built in the best harmony and with how much wise and
deep understanding my fiancée attends to the two motherless children.

According to Henry, the American widow was also everything he
looked for in a woman:

My fiancée is precisely that which I so ardently long for: a
person tested by deep suffering and as a consequence, sin-
cere, good-tempered, and though she is clement, decisive,
energetic and purposeful—with a great and true feeling for
art, wanting the best and seeking out the most beautiful.
Naturally we are no infants and have found each other in
a genuine, deep affection and our shared loneliness.

Both Henry's children, as well as several family members, had been
informed of the happy news by now.

I told the children the day before yesterday. At first they
were a bit quiet and then they were happy in a very moving way and such warmth issued from their dear hearts.
They spend a lot of time with my fiancée. They are becoming better acquainted all the time and hopefully growing

fonder too. I am genuinely amazed by the amount of
dependency and trust Marlisa has already developed for
her; with Heiner things are becoming easier and simpler.
My nearest relatives—the only people aside from you
who know of my engagement—have welcomed my fiancée with open arms, this after a long correspondence. As
I already wrote, they met in Dresden and there they grew
closer harmoniously. My oldest brother is coming here
tomorrow. My sister had to return to Berlin today. She,
too, was very taken by my fiancée and the great inner distinction of this unique woman.

He hoped the governess would also agree to put aside her *"pronon-
cierte Aversion gegen Ausländer"*—her "pronounced dislike of foreigners"—for the sake of the children, Henry wrote. He once again assured
her, perhaps unnecessarily, that his fiancée would raise the children
completely in the spirit and with the love their own mother had given
them and that they were in complete agreement about this. The wedding would probably take place in very closed circles the following April
in Paris, where his fiancée owned a house. In the meantime, the engagement should be kept secret until the widow's second year of mourning
had passed. The news would not be made public until February or
March for this reason.

***

In his hope-filled letter, the German prince might not have been cor-
rect about his betrothed's age or the high regard her family enjoyed in
America. But in one aspect he had aptly characterized Allene: she was
indeed downright lonely.

After her transatlantic journey in the spring of 1927, Allene had
stayed with her old friend Olive Greville, who had been party to her

marriage to Anson from the very start. But she couldn't stay with the Grevilles in England endlessly and so traveled on to Paris over the summer with the idea of building a new life there, like so many Americans who had something to run away from. She needed a new house for this, one that wouldn't constantly remind her of the person she'd rather have been in Paris with.

At the end of the summer, she walked around the elegant mansion that was to become hers, a grand house on the Rue Barbet-de-Jouy, for the first time. The house was in the seventh arrondissement, on the left bank of the Seine, where rich Americans with artistic tendencies had traditionally banded together. Around the corner, in the Rue de Varenne, lived the now elderly but still very successful writer Edith Wharton. Allene's house had been built during the short reign of Emperor Napoleon III for the then Count of Montebello and now belonged to his granddaughter.

Albertine de Montebello had been known in her youth as "one of the loveliest, most charming, most intelligent women Paris could boast of" and had hosted a renowned and fashionable political salon at the Rue Barbet for years. But this aging *comtesse* was yet another who found herself forced to sell her family possessions, due to lack of money and high taxes, to the Americans rolling in dollars who had alighted upon Paris like a swarm of noisy locusts. Americans who then thoroughly modernized their new possessions, because the French may have had patents on good taste and culture, but—the expats felt—they didn't have a clue about bathrooms and other modern American amenities.

And yet it seems it wasn't the location, the evocative history, or even the charm of the house, decorated generously with little cherubs and flowers, that was the decisive factor for Allene. It was the house number: 33, Allene's lucky number. This was a hangover from Jamestown, where an entrepreneurial tradesman had run a successful clothing business with the appropriate name of Proudfit at 33 Main Street. To advertise, he'd had trees and rocks painted with a double three for miles around and had even managed to claim the digits as a telephone number.

Allene hadn't taken much with her when she ran away as a pregnant eighteen-year-old, but she'd always kept the double three as her lucky number. Although raised Presbyterian, in this she showed herself to be as superstitious as the majority of her otherwise-so-modern compatriots—there still weren't any thirteenth floors in New York. And as believers fall back on their religions in difficult times, so the knocked-about Allene fell back on hers: a house with the number 33 on the front door had to bring her the luck she so desperately needed.

In early October 1927, almost to the day when Teddy would have turned thirty, she signed the purchase agreement. A few days later, she unveiled a memorial on the spot of her son's crash in Masnières, offered to her by the townspeople as thanks for her contribution to their village's reconstruction. The boys' school named after Teddy opened that same day. On the plaque announcing that the school had been built in memory of "their son," Allene and Anson were once again united in marble.

***

Sure enough, just a few months after Allene began a radical modernization of the house at 33 Rue Barbet-de-Jouy, she made the acquaintance of a handsome diplomat working at the German embassy in the nearby Rue de Lille. And he—how transparent fate can be!—also had a double three in his name, since Henry bore the aristocratic title of Prince Heinrich Reuss the Thirty-Third.

Henry had the Reuss family's remarkable habit of naming all their sons Heinrich to thank for the XXXIII in his name. The numbering began anew at the start of each century to distinguish them from one another. Aside from this, they were each given a nickname that was a variant of their given name. In this way, Henry's older brother went through life as Heino, his younger as Henrico, and his son—whose official title was Heinrich Prince Reuss II, because he was the second Reuss prince to be born that century—was called Heiner.

Henry didn't need the lucky number in his name to charm the rich but solitary American widow. He was known as a handsome and charming man. Once, when his German family could still lay serious claim to the Dutch throne—this because their relative Queen Wilhelmina threatened to remain childless—the Dutch had openly expressed their preference of him over his older, not particularly intelligent brother. During their eight-day visit to the Netherlands in 1908, Henry was enthusiastically welcomed as "intelligent, good-looking and artistically minded"—in all respects the ideal candidate for the throne.

That kingship never came to be, since against all expectation Wilhelmina managed to produce a daughter a year later. But Henry was still handsome. In short, Allene had found herself a seven-years-younger and very presentable husband, who, like her, was very well traveled—during his diplomatic career he'd been posted in Japan and Australia—and shared her great love of art. Aside from this—no mean feat for a girl who had taken her first steps in a livery stable in Jamestown—after the wedding she became one of the first Americans ever to be able to call herself a princess.

And finally—and perhaps this was the most important thing of all—with Henry and his motherless children, she would again have a family she could rightly call her own.

***

Incidentally, in his letter to the governess, Henry saved for last what could have been the most important detail for him: the financial consequences. In other words, money, something of which the prince had a chronic shortage.

Like most aristocratic German families, the Reusses had become impoverished since the end of the world war. After the collapse of the German front and the humiliating flight of Kaiser Wilhelm II in November 1918, a revolution had broken out that had toppled monarchies like domino pieces. Under the Weimar Republic that replaced the fragmented empire, aristocrats had to forfeit almost all their privileges and a large part of their land, which had traditionally provided their income.

For Henry's family, there was also this unfortunate circumstance: the family estate, Trebschen, was located in Posen, a province in the northeastern corner of the former empire. As a consequence of the Treaty of Versailles, in which Germany was forced to give up a large part of its territory, this province came to lie right next to the Polish border. The once-wealthy area soon emptied out and became impoverished, and by the time Henry met Allene, the Reuss brothers could hardly keep their heads above water. Everything they owned that could be sold was already gone, what was left of their land had been mortgaged to the hilt, and the house itself, which had been a real pleasure ground before the war, was now so dilapidated that their sister, who lived with her reasonably solvent husband in Stonsdorf, no longer wanted to visit with her family.

Henry made ends meet with difficulty in Paris, where he had taken up his old profession of diplomacy after being seriously wounded in the war on the Russian front. But the children, who had become his responsibility after the death of their mother, still lived in the crumbling Trebschen with his older brother, simply because Henry didn't have enough money to send them to a decent boarding school. What's more, his lack of money was exacerbated by his desire to keep up the life of luxury he felt his position afforded him the right to, and by the fact that he sometimes entertained himself with drinking and gambling—as was well known in Parisian diplomatic circles.

But a permanent end would come to all of these worries, Henry elatedly wrote to the governess after his future marriage had become a public fact in the spring of 1929:

> From next year onwards, I can finally give my children a better education than what has been possible so far in the remove countryside—supplemented with all kinds of healthy, practical matters of the modern time. One of my dearest wishes fulfilled so much sooner than I'd hoped. Languages, music, arts and sport, lots of sport!
>
> Likewise in the deepest confidence, I would like to say, that as far as I can predict, there will be major changes at Trebschen—probably during the coming year.

His future wife had promised to pay off the loans the family had taken out against the estate, according to Henry, and to have the house and the surrounding park renovated. After this, his eldest brother would have a comfortable home again, and even Henry's sister—whom the governess was very fond of—would be able to come back and stay with her family. But the governess had to stay mum about all this, of course, for the time being, since, as he wrote, "these affairs are being drawn up and considered at this time in a most careful, legal fashion, in this and all other respects." In brief, negotiations were still in full swing.

Allene must have realized herself, however lonely and infatuated she might have been, that her German prince charming hadn't courted her only for her pretty blue eyes and maternal instinct. Later, a friend of hers would describe the way she called a spade a spade during a joint visit to the former German emperor Wilhelm II, who lived in exile in Doorn in the Netherlands:

> During her engagement to Prince Henry of Reuss, they were dining with the Emperor Wilhelm II at Doorn

when the Kaiser, whose manners were always atrocious, demanded, not at all sotto voce: "What can a Prince of Reuss get out of marriage with an American?" Allene replied quite as audibly: "Sir, his bread and butter." And the Emperor did not pursue the topic further.

But Allene didn't doubt that a union partly forged upon financial motives could nevertheless be a happy one. Weren't almost all of the marriages between British aristocrats and American heirs or heiresses based on dollars? For many of them, such as her friends the Grevilles, the results had been more than satisfactory.

***

As was often the case in Allene's life, so closely followed by the society press, the news first broke in the *New York Times*: "Mrs. Burchard . . . is Reported Engaged to Prince Henry," the paper reported on October 28, 1928. Although by then the couple had appeared many times together in public at social events within the American colony in Paris, rumors about the imminent engagement had been categorically refuted. But reporters caught the whiff of a good story and closely followed all of Allene's movements from that moment on.

In December, the society widow traveled alone to New York—in all probability to arrange the business side of the forthcoming union. In early January, she returned to Europe again. From here she would continue on to Egypt, according to the newspapers, where she'd chartered a boat for a four-week cruise along the Nile. Among the seven guests she had invited were the British Lord and Lady Greville and the German prince with whom she'd been so often sighted the previous fall.

Less than two weeks after the luxurious *Indiana*—a floating palace, according to the papers—had set sail, an industrious news hunter at the *Washington Post* was quicker than his peers at the *Times*. "Prince is to Marry 300 000 Widow" ran the headline. Inaccurate as the report was—in reality, Allene was many times richer, of course—it sent the message to the home front that she had picked up the pieces of her life again and was living it to the full.

The day after that, the *New York Times* extensively covered the fairy tale of the tragic New York widow who'd been kissed awake by a *real* prince in an article richly illustrated with photographs. That this was indeed a fairy tale—although undoubtedly an unintentional one—was further emphasized by the pictures the couple put at the newspaper's disposition. In particular, the pictures of the now-blond, heavily made-up, and retouched Allene were so flattering that she was barely recognizable to her friends and acquaintances.

Allene's fourth wedding took place as planned on April 10 in her home on the Rue Barbet. The bride was given away by an acquaintance from the American embassy; apart from that, Henry's two brothers were the only other witnesses at the ceremony. His children weren't there— perhaps they hadn't come to such excellent terms with their new mother as he had earlier suggested—but they were taken along on the honeymoon, during which the brand-new family toured America in grand style. On the program were a visit to Sing Sing prison and its electric chair, the festive reopening of the St. Regis Hotel in New York, and a lunch at the Princeton Club organized in honor of the prince's visit.

The German prince accepted the respect for his status with visible pleasure, as a society reporter rather maliciously remarked, "Prince Henry was apparently not displeased with the concern his presence incited." It was true that the prince was "not at all bad looking, but somewhat more youthful than his wife," the item continued even more maliciously.

***

That summer, Trebschen's debts disappeared as if by magic, and a large-scale renovation of the estate was put into motion. Part of this was a new riding stable, designed by Henry himself. But during Allene's first visit to Germany in July 1929, she discovered that her husband might not have fully informed her of the degree of benevolence with which his family would greet her.

The German aristocracy may have lost practically all of its money and power, but it had given up none of its arrogance and snobbery. In general, the fact that one of their own had been driven by circumstances to marry so far beneath himself was experienced as an outrage. Allene's new in-laws weren't at all interested in the "great inner distinction" they'd attributed to her according to Henry's letter a year earlier. She was, as a relative said, not at all welcome in the family. They continued to blatantly speak German in Allene's presence even though they knew their new family member didn't understand a word of it.

But the greatest disappointment for Allene was undoubtedly her relationship with Henry's fourteen-year-old daughter, in whom she had hoped to find a new Greta. Marlisa used every opportunity she had to show that she wanted nothing, absolutely nothing, to do with her stepmother. Her own mother, Princess Viktoria Margarethe of Prussia, was Wilhelm II's niece and had been considered among Europe's highest nobility. How could this overly made-up, smoking American with her noisy friends ever think she could follow in her mother's aristocratic footsteps?

At first, Allene, optimistic as ever, didn't allow her fairy tale to be taken away from her. Of course Henry's family and children still had to get used to the new situation, and trust and love needed time to grow. And to demonstrate once again how serious she was in her resolve to do everything she could to make her husband happy—and without a doubt to prevent too many visits to Trebschen in the future—at the end of the summer she bought a romantic country house at Fontainebleau, around eighteen miles southeast of Paris.

Château de Suisnes had been built in 1684 as a hunting lodge for a mistress of Louis XIV, the Sun King. During the nineteenth century, it had come into the possession of explorer Louis-Antoine de Bougainville, who built an observatory and an artificial grotto and landscaped its seventeen-acre park with the beautiful Yerres River running through it. In these idyllic surroundings, Henry, who had set about painting fanatically during their Egyptian cruise and their American honeymoon, would finally have the time and space to indulge his lifelong artistic ambitions.

The fact that the landscape resembling the Swiss-Italian alps with which Henry covered the walls of the north salon in the Château de Suisnes the following winter could hardly be classified as great art can't have escaped even the love-stricken Allene. Her taste was too well developed due to the years she'd spent traveling the world with Anson and collecting art; she'd also been involved with the renowned Metropolitan Museum of Art for too long. But the many-foot-long wall painting was certainly unique, and, more important, painting kept her youthful husband occupied and distracted him from the alarming newspaper headlines that would soon overshadow their married life.

***

It began as a storm does: a gentle rumbling on the horizon in a still-sunlit landscape. On September 3, 1929—Allene's marriage was just six months old, and she was busy with the purchase of Château de Suisnes—share prices on Wall Street reached the highest level in history. This rendered Allene, whose fortune was almost entirely in American shares, even wealthier than before.

A year earlier, in the summer of 1928, an unexplained fall in prices had caused brief panic at the stock exchange, but the prices had soon risen again, setting new records. And America had peacefully continued settling into the "new era of prosperity" President Calvin Coolidge had promised his fellow Americans in 1927.

But halfway through October 1929, the stock market in New York again began to waver, just like the previous time, ostensibly out of the blue. Tense days followed, even though everyone expected the situation to rapidly stabilize, if at a slightly lower level than previously. But on October 24, the day that would later be known as "Black Thursday," the market went into a rapid and relentless nosedive, taking everything and everyone down with it. Desperate investors tried to fob off large portfolios of shares on errand boys for a few cents, entire fortunes evaporated, and dozens of despairing bankers jumped to their deaths from their luxurious offices.

The cause of the stock market crash was actually the same as all the other financial crises in the history of Wall Street: greed and sleight of hand with money. Now, too, speculators, financiers, and banking institutions turned out to have kept prices artificially high for years on end. Shares were offered against a small down payment; the rest of the amount could be paid off later from the profit made on them. But now with share prices dropping, there was no question of profits; only the debts were left, and the entire flimflam system collapsed like a house of cards.

The American colony in Paris was in the grip of anxiety and astonishment. Most of the expatriates took the first boat home to save what could still be saved. If they could no longer obtain enough cash to pay for their travel, they tried to sell off their French possessions for next to nothing—with revealing advertisements in the real estate publications as a result:

> For Sale, Cheap, Nice, Old Chateau, 1 hr. from Paris; original boiseries, 6 New Baths. Owner Forced Return New York Wednesday. MUST HAVE IMMEDIATE CASH. Will Sacrifice.

On November 12, a little less than three weeks after Black Thursday, Allene also boarded a ship for New York. At that moment, share prices on Wall Street, and with them their capital, had already lost a third of their value. Immediately upon arrival, she put the large city villa on Park Avenue and Birchwood, the country house in Locust Valley, on the market. In January 1930, when the market had calmed down somewhat and the worst seemed to be over, a Chicago businessman made an offer for Birchwood that was deemed good enough to be accepted. With this, Anson's house—the place where Allene had spent the happiest years of her life—disappeared from her possession for good.

Anyone thinking or hoping that the worst was over would be disappointed. From April onward, share prices continued to plunge unabated. The United States' total industrial production was reduced by half; a quarter of the population was already unemployed. A further eight hundred American banks collapsed. The construction cranes that had dominated New York's skyline since time immemorial came to a standstill, and apple sellers appeared on the city's street corners—former stockbrokers in expensive but already worn coats who tried to support themselves by selling fruit.

Improvised shantytowns of wood and cardboard sprang up among the rocky outcrops in Central Park, lived in by people who no longer even had a roof above their heads. And in the middle of this "echoing tomb," as F. Scott Fitzgerald described the crisis-hit New York, stood the new Empire State Building, the tallest building in the world, empty—as though to mock the megalomania and greed that had brought the city to its knees.

***

At some point in that cheerless, hopeless winter of 1930–1931, Allene finally managed to get rid of her vastly expensive mansion on Park Avenue. In its place, she bought an apartment in a building a little farther up that had become almost as much a concrete symbol of the crisis as the Empire State Building. Like the Empire State Building, 740 Park, on the corner of Park Avenue and Seventy-First Street, also had the bad luck to have been designed at the zenith of prosperity and completed at its nadir. The building was supposed to have been the magnum opus of Rosario Candela, a Sicilian immigrant who had come to America as a teenager and evolved into the New York upper class's architect of choice during the boom years.

In March 1929, construction had started on what was to be the most expensive and most exclusive apartment complex in New York. Most of the thirty-one apartments in the seventeen-story building were big enough to compete with detached houses in terms of space and proportions. They had their own halls, servants' wings, built-in refrigerators, telephone and radio sockets, marble floors, bronze window frames, fireplaces, and cedar closets to keep away moths. The basement was outfitted with rooms for chauffeurs, its own post office, laundry, storage, and wine cellars.

But when the building was completed in October 1930, there was almost no one left who wanted or was able to pay for all that luxury. In the spring of 1931, Allene was one of the very last buyers, and even she could only afford a relatively small apartment on Seventy-First Street, the darkest and least attractive side of the building. The many remaining empty apartments were simply rented, for a fraction of what their normal value would have been.

Shortly after this depressing house exchange, in April 1931, Allene took Henry to the city where she'd been raised. Jamestown hadn't even needed the Great Depression to fall into decline. Around 1910, the rise of the automobile had put an end to Chautauqua's brief popularity as a vacation destination. The large wooden hotels on the lake had as good as vanished—most of them had burned to the ground, perhaps in fires set intentionally to reap the insurance premiums.

In subsequent years, the furniture industry had kept local business going in Jamestown, but now that the American economy had practically come to a standstill, one factory after the next was forced to close its doors. Even Proudfit, the eighty-year-old clothing shop on Main Street, could no longer be saved by its lucky number; shortly before Allene's visit, it had filed for bankruptcy. Jamestown had returned to what it had once been: a quiet and actually rather ugly town, surrounded by endless woods, where lumberjacks, hunters, and farmers came to purchase their supplies.

On July 8, 1932, Wall Street finally hit rock bottom. Share values were now nearly 90 percent less than they had been in September 1929. A few weeks later, on a stuffy summer's day, a chambermaid at The Pierre hotel on Sixty-First Street detected a strange smell coming from a room with a "Do Not Disturb" sign on its door. A little while later, the lifeless body of Morton Colton Nichols, Allene's second husband, was discovered. He had sniffed chloroform, taken cyanide, and then hanged himself, and had already been dead for a few days.

According to a family member—probably his second wife, from whom he was long estranged—persistent stomachache was the cause of the suicide. And bellyache is something Morton Nichols would certainly have had. After his death, it was discovered that he hadn't just lost his own money in the crash but had run through the entire family trust fund, including the fortune of his niece Ruth Nichols, who had become a national celebrity as one of the first female pilots—"The Flying Debutante."

***

Poor Henry. It was as if the devil was playing games with him. The losses and disappointments had piled up for as long as he could remember. First the Dutch throne, whipped from under his family's nose by the birth of Princess Juliana. Then the war, so ignominiously and unfairly lost in the eyes of members of the German aristocracy. Then the revolution, which had taken from him and his family all that they had considered their birthright for centuries: political power, social status, and money.

And when he finally thought he might have gotten the better of fate by marrying a wealthy American, less than half a year later, the stock market crash and the rapid depreciation of Allene's fortune began to rub all the shine off their fairy-tale marriage. Even his artistic career had ended in failure: an exhibition Allene had organized in the prestigious New York Wildenstein gallery had drawn neither buyers nor admiring critics, and his work had received the designation "painfully wrought."

Allene herself, scratched and scraped by fate as she was, could handle the loss. She had gone from incredibly rich to a little less wealthy. Her Victorian childhood had given her enough self-discipline, and her marriage to Anson enough financial savvy, to be able to bear a blow like this one. As she once complained in a letter, "There is so much sadness and trouble in the world, one's heart is torn all the time, also one's purse, but this life is a school." She cut back dramatically on her own spending, kept a keener-than-ever eye on her accounts, and economized on everything. She rented out her apartment on Park Avenue when she wasn't there and would buy a new hat instead of a new wardrobe. In her own words, "I think a hat most important for a woman, you can wear an old dress if the hat is new." But she still didn't sell her shares, and certainly not for a few cents to an errand boy.

For her highborn husband, on the other hand, the Great Depression was one setback too many. Henry sought refuge in drinking and gambling as of old, and in peevishness he unleashed on his wife more and more frequently in public. He may have once come into the world with a proverbial silver spoon in his mouth, but no one could say he had been born under a lucky star.

9

The Fifth Man

Rache, Rache, und nochmals Rache! Revenge, revenge, and once again revenge. That was what Henry and his brothers had sworn in 1924 as they revealed a monument in Ostritz, near Trebschen, for the Germans killed in the war. Revenge for the lost war, which they were convinced could have been won if the country hadn't been sabotaged, inside out, by international Jewry. Revenge for the downfall of the German empire and their monarchy. And in particular revenge for the Treaty of Versailles, which had condemned their country to an existence as Europe's hapless pauper.

At the time, the United States was the only nation that had rejected the peace treaty signed in Versailles on June 28, 1919. The Americans felt, in part, that the reparations the Germans had to pay as instigators of the war were too draconian; the restrictions imposed on the country were too humiliating. They seemed to be the only ones to realize that you always have to give a person or a nation the opportunity to be a good loser.

During the postwar years, it was mainly Americans who had dared to invest heavily in ravaged and traumatized Germany. Thanks to them, the German economy had slowly been able to scramble to its feet again over the course of the 1920s. But when those same Americans were forced to hastily recoup their money after the 1929 stock market crash, the bottom fell out of Germany's still-fragile economic market. The Great Depression, which had spread across the planet like a viscous oil slick, hit the world hard but nowhere as hard as it did in Germany.

Unemployment figures shot up, the government was powerless, and the battered country was hit by a paralyzing malaise in which extremist political ideals could easily take root—ideals such as those of Austrian-born Adolf Hitler, who in 1920 set up the *Nationalsozialistische Deutsche Arbeiterpartei* (NSDAP), the National Socialist German Workers' Party, in Munich, along with a group of other war vets. He said everything many Germans, embittered and robbed of their self-respect, wanted to hear: that the Jews were to blame for everything, that the Treaty of Versailles was criminal, and that the politicians of the Weimar Republic were traitors who had thrown away their country.

At first, the German aristocracy wanted little to do with the noisy demagogue from Munich. But Hitler successfully managed to give the impression that the former elite would rise again to eminence under his rule and, more important, that he was their only hope to exorcise the Bolshevik threat from the east. From 1930 onward, more and more German aristocrats began to sign up as members of the NSDAP.

Allene's husband, Henry Reuss, was not yet a member—probably because he was a Freemason and the national socialist movement refused admission to that group's members. But when the NSDAP became the largest party in 1932 and Adolf Hitler managed to secure the position of Reich chancellor, beginning a large-scale Nazification of Germany, Allene's husband tried all kinds of ways to forge an alliance with his fatherland's New Order.

In November 1933, living temporarily in Berlin, Henry wrote a letter in which he offered to work as an unpaid volunteer for Hitler's right hand, Heinrich Himmler, at the Schutzstaffel, the NSDAP's paramilitary organization. "The SS liaison staff would suit me," he wrote, "leaving aside my affinities with the SS." He omitted to mention that the French government had asked him to remain in his own country for the time being because of his, for a diplomat, rather fanatically vented fascist ideas.

***

Later Allene would tell her friends that it was mainly her husband's political views that had led to the schism in their marriage. All totalitarian systems, whether communist or fascist, were alien to her—as a true-blue American and believer in a democratic republic, she couldn't imagine any other political system. Henry even caused problems with the household staff. At a certain point, the staff, some of whom were Jewish, refused to wear livery with the Reuss coat of arms in protest of their employer's virulent anti-Semitism.

In any case, Henry's overtures seemed to have little effect on the Nazis. Now that Hitler held absolute power in Germany, he no longer needed the aristocracy to make him or his party socially acceptable, and the letter sent in November 1933 was never answered. In August 1934— Hitler had made short shrift of practically all of his political opponents less than five weeks earlier during a series of political executions, the bloody "Night of the Long Knives"—Henry tried again. He offered to put the Trebschen estate at the disposal of the esteemed führer, whom he presumed must be tired by "his burdens and responsibilities of the state," in order for him to catch his breath. The estate was relatively close to Berlin, Henry wrote temptingly, and yet remote enough to guarantee the leader of the German Reich privacy and peace and quiet. "It's very quiet but the most important thing is that one sleeps wonderfully here!"

The Nazis also disregarded this generous offer. And because Henry was no longer welcome in France or in the Rue Barbet, in the fall of 1934, out of desperation, he moved into his sister's castle in Stonsdorf.

There, to while away the hours, he painted a kind of Alpine landscape on the walls of the dining room, just as he'd decorated the drawing room in the Château de Suisnes.

As was her custom, Allene traveled to New York in October for a couple of months to settle her affairs and see her friends. Contrary to previous years, she boarded the cruise liner without a husband, a detail the ever-alert American press hounds immediately noted. In particular, Maury Paul—the most famous society reporter of the period, feared for his sharp tongue—wrote openly in his Cholly Knickerbocker columns about the Reusses' marital crisis, with clear knowledge of the affair:

> Henry had been a flat failure as a husband, judged from all angles, but Allene kept her nose tilted proudly and declined to confirm stories of marital discord.

Head proudly held high or not, somewhere in that dark, crisis-ridden winter, Allene must have realized that the fairy tale in which she played an American princess was over. Although she clung to her revised birth year of 1876, in fact she was already several years past sixty, and all the beauty specialists, plastic surgeons, and couturiers in the world could no longer disguise the fact that the days when she was commonly recognized as a beauty were now consigned to the past. The illusion of being the kind of beloved wife she'd been to Anson had been destroyed by the many often-humiliating scenes she'd had with Henry. Her dream of becoming a mother again also lay in pieces. Although her stepson, Heiner, still accepted her care and attention, his sister, Marlisa, still treated her with icy contempt.

To make matters worse, Allene's brief illusion of finding happiness with Henry had cost her buckets of money. A divorce would undoubtedly cost much more—and this at the very moment when her finances were already under serious pressure from the economic crisis, which dragged on and by now had reduced half of America to poverty. Things were going so badly for the apartment complex on Park Avenue that its proprietors had been forced a year earlier to hand over the still mainly empty building to an insurance company, an event that transformed its owners into renters.

But there was a reason Allene's motto was "Courage all the time." If there was one thing she could call herself a real expert in by now, it was cutting her losses. On July 26, 1935, Allene's secretary in Paris, Alice Brown, announced that Allene and Henry were separating. For Henry, this was the perfect moment for a new start: not only had he been accepted as an NSDAP member almost two months earlier, but his eldest brother had died, leaving him Trebschen and whatever else remained in the family's possession.

As for Allene, she simply refused to comment. In fact, no comment was necessary. That summer and fall, she frequently appeared with a new companion at her side—one who was even younger and more handsome than the previous one—her eyebrows raised provocatively as in her younger years on Lake Chautauqua.

***

In a certain sense, the man who would become Allene's fifth and final husband was a kind of legacy from Henry. Or better still, from Trebschen, where Allene's experiences had primarily been ungratifying. She had made friends with one of Henry's neighbors, who was almost as much a pariah to the German aristocracy as she herself. Armgard zur Lippe-Biesterfeld lived in a rather dilapidated former hunting lodge on the Reckenwalde lake, a few miles from Trebschen. She was a fanatical horse lover and an avid smoker and was renowned for not giving a damn. A widow, she now always appeared in public with her five-years-younger horse trainer, a Russian exile by the name of Alexis Pantchoulidzew.

"Tschuli" as the Reckenwalde horseman was known, came from a prominent Russian family and had trained at the Saint Petersburg Page Corps, the most elite military academy in czarist Russia. After the revolution in 1917 and the subsequent civil war, like many others, he had been forced to flee the country and had ended up with the zur Lippe family in 1922. The former students of the Page Corps were known to maintain close contact with each other in exile, and the chance is therefore great that he was the person who introduced Allene to Pavel Pavlovitch Kotzebue—or Paul, as he was known in French.

Just like Tschuli, Paul had been in the Page Corps and after that had been employed in the czarist court as a cavalryman and bodyguard; both had fought on the side of the counterrevolutionaries in the civil war, and both—made destitute by the communist seizure of power— had been forced to seek refuge in Europe. But there was an unusual story attached to Paul, since in March 1917, right after the revolution, he had for a short time guarded none other than Nicholas II, the newly deposed czar. Allene may have been able to read about her future husband in 1917, since he had given an extensive interview about this to the *New York Times*.

***

The reason the revolutionary government had entrusted thirty-three-year-old Paul Kotzebue with guarding the most important prisoner in the country in early March 1917 probably had something to do with a youthful error. Once, when he was still one of Czarina Alexandra Feodorovna's bodyguards, Paul had appeared at a masked New Year's ball dressed as a woman and turned the heads of all the men present. When the identity of the elegant guest who had jumped into a waiting sleigh just before midnight and disappeared without a trace was later revealed, he was fired from the court on the spot.

Paul worked for a few years as personal assistant to Prime Minister Pyotr Stolypin, who was murdered in 1911 by a political opponent. In 1912, Nicholas II took pity on Paul and hired him again. He was appointed captain in the czar's family's favorite residence, the Alexander Palace, near Saint Petersburg. There he witnessed the glory days of Rasputin, a faith healer originally from Siberia whose help was called in regarding the poor health of Alexei, the heir to the throne. In those days, Russia abounded with rumors about the sexual debauchery of the miracle doctor—Rasputin held the view that in order to regret one's sins, it was first necessary to have committed a lot of them—and the unhealthy power he exercised at court, particularly over the czarina.

Meanwhile, the world war that had broken out in 1914 ended dramatically for the czarist empire, already exhausted from its earlier war with Japan. The underfed and barely armed Russian soldiers didn't stand a chance against the slick German fighting machine, and dissatisfaction with the czarist administration and hatred of Rasputin grew by the day. On the night of December 29–30, 1916, a group of aristocrats tried to turn the tide by murdering the faith healer, to the deep sorrow of the czar and his family. Alexandra had him declared a saint, and Nicholas II carried the monk's embalmed body in his own arms to its last resting place in a chapel on the outskirts of the palace gardens.

But Rasputin's death came too late to restore the trust of the Russian population in its leaders. A few weeks later, food riots broke out in Saint Petersburg, and soon afterward in the rest of the country, too. On March 15, 1917, Nicholas II found himself forced to give up the throne. Together with his family and a number of faithful followers, he waited for history to take its course in his residential palace, guarded by Paul, a man the provisional government felt would be sympathetic to the revolutionaries' cause since he had once been fired from the czarina's regimental guard.

Later, various members of Nicholas II's court would testify that this certainly wasn't the case:

The new War Minister, Guchkov appointed Captain
Kotzebue of the Cavalry, Commandant of the Palace, hoping that he would act like a real jailer, as he had promised,
but, Kotzebue, to his honor, accepted this post only that
he might be able to come to the help of the prisoners and
mitigate the hardships of their existence as far as possible.
He allowed them to have uncensored correspondence, sent
off telephone messages for them, bought for them secretly
the things they needed.

A reporter from the *New York Times* who, later that month, managed to penetrate the palace almost completely cut off from the outside
world, noticed how respectfully the head jailer behaved toward his prisoners. While other guards made a sport of speaking as scornfully to the
fallen monarch as possible—calling him "Citizen Nikolai Romanov" or
"Little Nikolai"—Paul addressed him as "Former Emperor" and spoke
with evident fondness of him and his family.

The former emperor was in good health and relatively good spirits,
despite occasional fits of crying, Paul told the reporter. He took daily
walks in the garden with his wife's ladies-in-waiting and made himself
useful clearing snow, "which he enjoys greatly." He also showed a boyish
interest in everything written about him, in particular in the foreign
press. Young Prince Alexei was in reasonable health but cried terribly
when he heard his father had given up the throne. And the czarina was
ill, although according to her empathetic guard it was mainly because
her heart had been broken: "Her real malady is from the heart."

The American reporter was clearly impressed by the handsome
Russian and described Paul as the height of civility and courtly manners: "Youthful and urbane, an officer of the guard type, speaking perfect French and English." They got along so well together that they
visited the improvised grave of Rasputin—"the unintending parent of
the revolution," in the journalist's words—together. They found the

chapel sullied and soiled, the rock face next to it covered in insulting inscriptions such as "Here lies Rasputin, foulest of men, the shame of the Romanov dynasty."

According to a family chronicle about the Kotzebues that was published later, this wasn't in fact Paul's first visit to the monk's final resting place. An eyewitness would say that the revolutionary government had given him the rather unsavory task, earlier that month, of visiting the tomb with a yardstick to check whether the rumor about the legendary size of Rasputin's member was true:

> Although the body had been embalmed, the stench was so strong that Count Kotzebue, an elegant officer (he later became count), who had been given this horrible task, told me he thought he would pass out.

The interview with Paul that Allene may have read was published in the *New York Times* on March 27, 1917, under the headline "Ex-Czar, Guarded, Has Fits of Crying." The article ended with the statement that security at the palace had been stepped up in connection with rumors about potential escape attempts by the czar. Indeed, members of the Kotzebue family later recounted that Paul had tried to bring Nicholas II, disguised as a palace guard, to safety.

At the last minute—the boat that would have taken him to a steamship in the Gulf of Finland was ready and waiting on the Neva River—the former czar, who may have been a poor ruler but was a solid family man, decided that he couldn't leave without his family. It was a decision that would cost him his life. The revolutionary government no longer trusted Paul and relieved him of his role at the end of March. In August 1917, the Romanovs were transported to Siberia. A little less than a year later, they were moved to Ekaterinburg, where they were executed in July 1918.

***

At the time the czar's family was being slaughtered, Russia was in the grips of a civil war that the Red Army would win in 1920, led by Communist Vladimir Lenin. Paul; his mother; his older sister, Marie; his older brother, Alexander; and Alexander's wife (born Countess Tolstoy) were among the hundreds of thousands of czarists who fled their motherland.

Like most exiles, the Kotzebues first settled in Berlin with the firm conviction that the international community would never tolerate the establishment of a socialist state and that they'd be able to return to their homeland at any moment. That hope evaporated in 1922, when the communist Soviet Union was founded and then recognized by one nation after the next. Paul and his sister—their mother had died in the meantime—left with the great stream of refugees for France, which had traditionally counted as a second homeland for Russian artists and aristocrats. Their brother ended up in Switzerland, where he was able to set up a banking company with what was left of the family fortune.

During the 1920s and the first part of the '30s, Paul and his sister seem to have led unremarkable lives in a modest apartment on the Avenue du Président-Wilson in Paris. Neither of them married, and neither of them played much of a role in the Russian exile community. As far as can be ascertained, Paul was in contact only with his former fellow students from the Page Corps. When the brother and sister went to New York in November 1934, they told the immigration service they were fifty and fifty-two years old, respectively, and without profession or nationality.

What Paul did have, though, was an aristocratic title: in 1933, a cousin of his father's, Count Dimitri Kotzebue-Pilar von Pilchau, had transferred his title to Paul with permission of the imperial family in exile. Shortly thereafter he met the American princess whose fairy-tale marriage to German Prince Henry Reuss had ended in such public disappointment. She was clearly in need of a new life partner; he, in turn, could use a wife who would give him new status and would return to the Kotzebue family the respect they had once enjoyed in Russia.

***

On October 31, 1935, Allene was granted her second "Paris divorce." Less than half a year later, on March 4, 1936, she married Paul Kotzebue in a closed ceremony in the Russian church in Geneva, in the presence of Paul's brother, Alexander, and his sons, among others. News of Allene's fifth wedding was met with unsurprising mockery in both the American and the international press. "There is something of a perennial Cinderella about the Countess Kotzebue," wrote Maury Paul, rather gently by his standards—but he had a soft spot for his enterprising compatriot.

A leading columnist for the *Washington Post* wrote a derogatory comment about the remarkable wedding—which she would have found even more remarkable if she'd known that another two marriages took place prior to the three she named:

> Greatest example of name-changes leading to stark madness here is probably the case of the Countess Kotzebue, who before that was Princess Henry XXXIII of Reuss, and before that was Mrs. Anson Wood Burchard. Before that, it is probably fair to assume, she was a pranksome child who harassed her governess and teased the cat . . .

A scornful article also appeared in German and Dutch newspapers, titled "The Princess with the Record Number of Marriages." In that piece, Allene was portrayed as a rather calculating fortune and title hunter, aside from once—"the most captivating debutante in New

York" who continued her search for eternal happiness against her better judgement:

> It really is never too late. During the last year of her fourth marriage, Allene, who is now in her sixties, got to know Count Kotzebue in Paris, a BalticRussian emigré, descendent of a famous comedy player and nephew of the last Tsarist envoy in Washington. And with her ring-adorned hand she has reached for him for—how do we say it again?—for a union for life.

But the world could tease and mock as it liked—this time Allene knew what she was doing. This time no photographs of a smoothed-out, retouched bride were sent to the media to convince outsiders that New York's saddest widow had finally found happiness. This time Allene didn't need to launch a desperate charm offensive on her new in-laws. She was accepted by the Kotzebues, without reservation, for who she was: an older lady with a great fortune and a big heart, both of which she liked to share with other people.

No doubt Allene's seriously reduced—but, compared to the Kotzebues', still-substantial—wealth played a role in this marriage, too. There must have been a reason that, days after the wedding, Paul was added to the deed as joint owner of the house on Rue Barbet. But unlike his predecessor, the Russian saw no reason to treat his wife with scorn once he'd gained financial independence. "Paul was kindness itself, a gift so rare among men," a distant cousin characterized him.

Indeed, just as the gentle Russian had once dedicated himself to the care of the czar he was guarding, now he did the same for his twelve-years-older wife, whose life had been just as determined and marked by the history of the West as his had been by the East. Paul and Allene were both fate's castaways, each in their own way. Both had washed up in Paris, both of them had been through too much to still cherish great illusions or dreams, and both of them were determined to make the best of whatever was left.

***

Almost at the same time Allene was pledging eternal fidelity for the fifth time in a church in Geneva, on the other side of the world, the last tangible reminder of her first marriage was going up in flames.

Hostetter House on Raccoon Creek, which she and Tod had built and which Greta had bought back later because she had such fine childhood memories of it, had come back into Allene's possession following Greta's death. Since then it had stood empty for years in the dark woods west of Pittsburgh like a Victorian haunted house—its shutters closed, the chimney cold, the park around it full of cawing crows.

Allene employed a married couple living in the brick house behind it to take care of the property, ensuring that it wasn't broken into and that the "log cabin" remained exactly as it had been the last time Greta left it. The only function the building still had was as a beacon for ships maneuvering themselves up the Ohio River.

The caretakers had failed to take their own adopted daughter into account. After a row with her parents, she hid in one of the big house's bedrooms and built a fire. In no time, Hostetter House transformed into an inferno that could be seen from far and wide. The only parts to survive the sea of fire were the stone chimney and the basement where Tod had his wine cellars and the servants their lodgings.

The chimney was demolished that same year due to danger of collapse. The foundations in the dark woods soon became so overgrown that all that was left of the house was a slight elevation in the landscape. The underground corridors and rooms would be filled with bricks and rubble, necessary to bear the weight of an enormous power plant that was built on top of it. But that was a few years later, when the vindictiveness of men like Henry Reuss had cast the world into a new war that in many regards was even more horrific than its predecessor.

10

The Godmother

Bernhard was his name—Prince Bernhard zur Lippe-Biesterfeld in full, but to many of his friends he was simply "Biesterfeld" and to his adoring mother, Armgard, "Bernilo." This was also the name Allene called him, and she had done so since the first time she'd met him, in the summer of 1929, when the skies above her fourth marriage still looked relatively cloudless. Photos from the time show a very young Bernhard, wearing knickers and the round glasses that would later become his trademark, side by side with his neighbor Marlisa and the newlywed Reusses, Allene's curly-haired white dog playing happily around them.

A lot had happened since that carefree summer. The international economy had collapsed, dragging down with it Allene and Henry's marriage and what remained of German prosperity. Bernhard's father had died fairly unexpectedly, and his mother had been left practically penniless. His parents' home was on the verge of collapse; the land had been sold, and there was no money left for the law degree that had given Bernhard a good excuse for unbridled partying in Munich. He had nipped his career in the National Socialists' aviation department in the bud by crashing an airplane beyond repair almost instantly; his weak physical constitution had made him unsuited to other paramilitary factions.

His only option was to look for a job. In September 1935, Bernhard started work as an unpaid intern at the Paris branch of a German chemical company. Allene put him up, and they remained in touch in the intervening years. She liked to surround herself with young, cheerful people she could help a little in finding their way in life.

After just a few weeks in the offices of IG Farben, Bernhard came to the conclusion that he wasn't cut out to spend his days at a desk or work his way up from the bottom in the business world. His life of luxury in the beautiful home of his hospitable benefactor suited him incredibly well, though. "He was allowed to drive all her cars," his mother later explained with pride. He revised his ambitions in the customary manner. Wasn't marriage to a woman of wealth the age-old remedy for poverty-stricken aristocrats?

***

Later, the American press, never afraid to fatten a juicy story, would make the most of Allene's role in rescuing the Dutch monarchy. It was beyond dispute, of course, that the monarchy required rescuing. Halfway through the 1930s, it was widely known in diplomatic—and journalistic—circles that Queen Wilhelmina was having great trouble finding a husband for her daughter, Juliana. And since Juliana was the only person who could provide an heir to the throne, it could mean an end to the Dutch royal house.

In general, the problem was attributed to the princess's lack of external charms. But playing in the background, and perhaps even more dominant, was Wilhelmina's rather off-putting reputation among the aristocracy. The old queen was reputed to be provincial, humorless, and exceptionally economical, and eligible European princes told each other with a shudder how playing shuffleboard counted as the height of frivolity at the Hague court.

After years of fruitless searching, Dutch diplomats had given up hope. There weren't many suitable princes from Protestant houses. And now that Germany, the traditional supplier of aristocratic husbands, was coming back to life economically under Hitler's regime, potential fiancés were less than keen to seek their futures in the still-crisis-beset country next door. By now Juliana was over twenty-five, and after years of being dragged around Europe to no avail, she was no more attractive and certainly no more self-assured.

And then came Bernhard zur Lippe-Biesterfeld—in the colorful words of an American paper, "another obscure hall-room boy until lightning struck him, with the assist of an American heiress."

> The former Allene Tew of New York and Pittsburgh decided to back Bernhard for the jackpot prize . . . At the time the American princess entered Bernhard in the sweepstakes, he was trying to keep body and soul together as an auto salesman in a Paris branch of IG Farben . . . Of course she went along to mastermind the affair. For Bernhard was everything the Dutch princess was not: gay, debonair, worldly, dashing—and slim!

Bernhard may not have been a car salesman or a hall-room boy (bellhop), but he was certainly obscure—in any case in the eyes of the sleuthing Dutch diplomatic corps, who hadn't even known he existed, let alone ever considered him as suitable marriage material. The latter had to do with the fact that his parents' marriage had never been formally recognized because while his father may have been high nobility, his mother had never had a title of her own and was divorced at that. Armgard and her two sons' aristocratic credentials were, in fact, no more than meaningless consolation titles supplied by an uncle for the occasion.

From his relatives on his father's side—in which several cousins had already been felt out as potential candidates—Bernhard knew how desperate the situation around the Dutch royal house had become. And he decided, possibly egged on by Allene, to try his chances. Juliana may not have been pretty, but she was the daughter of possibly the richest woman in Europe. Marrying her would put an instant end to all of his worries and, equally important, those of his mother, whom he adored.

***

Bernhard's first documented attempt to meet the Dutch princess dated back to November 1935. On the advocacy of one of Wilhelm II's adjutants, he was able to attend a lunch at the house of John Loudon, the Dutch ambassador in Paris. But when the young intern asked his host how he could come into contact with Juliana and her mother, the host didn't respond. The Dutch may have been desperate, but they weren't desperate enough to want to pair their princess with a young man who'd shown up from nowhere, without demonstrable merit or even an academic degree.

A few months later, Bernhard was given a second chance. An aunt on his father's side tipped him off that in February 1936 the Dutch queen and her daughter would attend the Olympic Winter Games in Garmisch-Partenkirchen, a Bavarian resort town. He requested leave from his work, borrowed a car and some money from Allene, and drove to southern Germany, armed with his skis. On the way, he couldn't resist the temptation to make a stopover in Munich, where he'd had such a happy time as a student. He ran through all of Allene's money in no time and had to pass a hat among his bar friends to get together sufficient funds to continue his journey at the end of the evening.

And so it came about that Bernhard arrived late, but not too late, in snowy Garmisch. He managed to come into contact with Juliana on a ski run and charmed her mother and the ladies-in-waiting to the extent that a correspondence was started after the holiday. On March 8, 1936, from his garret on the Rue Barbet, Bernhard wrote his first letter to Juliana. It was six pages long and recounted, among other things, the wedding ceremony of his "aunt" Allene and Paul Kotzebue, which he'd just attended in Geneva. He had almost crashed his car on the misty alpine roads on the way, he wrote.

***

While their Rue Barbet housemate worked on his career in his wholly original manner, Allene and Paul spent their honeymoon in their favorite city, Rome. They rented an apartment in the ancient Palazzo Fani Mignanelli, which belonged to a couple they knew—the American banker Cécil Blunt and his aristocratic Italian wife, Anna Pecci, who enjoyed international fame as art collectors and patrons of modern artists like Salvador Dalí and Jean Cocteau. This Roman pied-à-terre, which Allene and Paul would also keep in the following years, was on the Piazza d'Aracoeli, a small square between the Capitoline Hill and Piazza Venezia.

After a few weeks in the Italian spring sun, the Kotzebues traveled on to New York. They were accompanied by Heiner Reuss, Allene's stepson from her former marriage. Henry's son was nineteen and had grown into a slender, humorous young man who was keen to please. To his father's dismay, he did not in any way fit the national-socialist ideal of tough masculinity that had become a standard in Germany, so following the divorce, he veered more and more toward "Mama," as he called his stepmother.

At the beginning of the summer, the trio returned to Paris, where in the meantime, houseguest Bernhard had made good progress in his quest to conquer a place in the world through the Dutch royal family. After a total of three visits lasting several days each—during which he had indeed become acquainted with the famed shuffleboard—on July 10, 1936, he asked for Juliana's hand in marriage.

The princess was now head over heels in love with the charming, worldly young man who had appeared in her life so unexpectedly. Wilhelmina, too, had received "a very good impression" of him, as she wrote to a diplomat. The fact that neither of them had yet met any of the potential husband's family members or friends was of little consequence given the relief that there was finally a serious candidate for Juliana's hand. "Beggars can't be choosers," as the Dutch ambassador in Berlin summed up the matter.

For the rest of the summer, frenzied plans were made behind the scenes to introduce Bernhard in the Netherlands and to establish a marriage contract. The prospective husband had already stated that he didn't want to be financially dependent on his wife after their wedding. On August 5, a constitutional amendment was shepherded through Dutch parliament in which it was laid down that a future prince consort would receive an annual income of a very respectable 200,000 gulden. Given that this sum could hardly come from national coffers already hit hard by the economic crisis, Juliana donated the money from her own income as heir to the throne.

Several days earlier, Allene had invited the Dutch queen and her ministers to Château de Suisnes to negotiate the marriage contract. The invitation was turned down—Allene's country house was too close to civilization, Wilhelmina thought. Instead, the parties met on August 13 in a remote hotel in the Bernese Highlands of Switzerland. Allene, Paul, and Bernhard, who'd driven there together, were met by a visibly nervous Juliana, who had a bad cold; her thrifty mother; and ministers who—given the prehistory—were undoubtedly hoping matters would be settled swiftly so they could resume their vacations.

Later, Paul Kotzebue would tell one of Bernhard's biographers how nerve-racking the atmosphere had been for the three long days during which Allene tried to get as good a price for her protégé as she could from Wilhelmina and the ministers. "Juliana, Bernhard, and I sat in the lobby of the hotel to wait until my wife returned," he said. "We didn't manage to conduct a polite conversation." It wasn't until the evening of August 15 that white smoke spiraled out of the negotiation room: an agreement had been reached.

The next day, the Kotzebues offered the Dutch delegation a farewell lunch in Lucerne. In the spirit of the festivities, Wilhelmina, normally a fervent teetotaler, deigned to take a very small sip of wine. She also refrained, with visible difficulty, from commenting when her daughter, in imitation of the rest of the cheerfully smoking company, suddenly lit up a cigarette, albeit rather clumsily.

***

The engagement of the Dutch princess was made public on September 8, 1936. It was considerably earlier than had been intended, but Bernhard and his mother clearly didn't want to run any risks that the union might be called off, and they'd had the news leaked through a journalist friend. The entire Netherlands celebrated, while Juliana and her mother met Armgard, Bernhard's mother, for the first time. She came to The Hague for the occasion and filled her role as future royal mother-in-law with panache.

Allene remained in the background during the celebrations. Within the Bernhard cult that was now developing, she was just an aunt with whom he'd happened to be lodging for career reasons when he'd lost his heart to Juliana. The fact that there was no family connection remained unnoticed. Just as it was in no one's interest to check the future husband's credentials now that one had finally been found, there was no reason to look into the woman he had been staying with.

And so Allene went down in Dutch history as Bernhard's somewhat mysterious American aunt, about whom little was known other than that she'd had a number of wealthy husbands and, as a consequence, had grown very rich. The presence of such a large fortune belonging to a "close relative" provided Bernhard with an aura of wealth missing from his own family, one he could really use. For his entire life, he would continue to deny having married for anything as vulgar as money. Nor did anyone bring up the article that had appeared half a year earlier in various Dutch newspapers under the headline "The Princess with the Record Number of Marriages."

The wedding took place on January 7, 1937, in The Hague. Guest of honor Allene adorned herself with a tiara that day that was apparently rather tight: to the horror of the aristocratic guests, she simply removed it during dinner and laid it on the table in front of her. As a wedding gift, the Kotzebues gave the couple an antique Russian icon, encased in gold, depicting Our Lady of Perpetual Help, a very fitting image given Allene's role in the establishment of the union.

And Allene continued to provide assistance, even during the couple's honeymoon. It soon became clear to Juliana that her young husband did not intend to give up the company of his bachelor friends or attractive women after the wedding. The Dutch princess had no idea how to make the most of herself as a woman. Her mother had sent her to her wedding night in flannel underwear. American women, on the other hand, were famous for leaving nothing to Mother Nature where their physical appearance was concerned, and Allene was no exception.

When the royal couple spent a week on the Piazza d'Aracoeli at the end of March, Allene, always softhearted when it came to the underdog, took it upon herself to give the Dutch woman more self-confidence. She had her beauty specialist come over to Europe on a boat from New York and made appointments with Worth and Molyneux, the two Parisian fashion houses where she was a regular customer herself. In early April, Juliana—who had lost several pounds on her honeymoon—was fitted with a new contemporary and, in particular, flattering wardrobe. The hastily shipped-over American beautician completed the metamorphosis of "a plump, placid, pleasant lass into an almost dashing young woman of the world," as the stylist told one newspaper.

Later, Wilhelmina, as frugal and averse to ostentation as ever, would have almost all of the clothes her daughter ordered from the Paris fashion houses sent back. In the meantime, Juliana's Parisian transformation, as remarkable as it was short-lived, was put down to Bernhard's influence, both by his biographers and himself. Like all good honeymoons, this one too ended in Paris where Bernhard promptly telephoned Aunt Allene. "What's the best fashion house at the moment? Lanvin?" he asked.

"No, Lanvin is passé," Countess Kotzebue cried. "Nowadays you need to be at Worth and Molyneux."

"Wonderful," said the prince, "would you like to go there with us tomorrow? We'll order a few things for Juliana that don't look like they've been made by the local dressmaker, eh?"

Nevertheless, Allene's efforts paid off—and very concretely, too, in the form of an heir to the throne who came into the world in late January 1938, exactly nine months after the Paris shopping spree, thus rescuing the Dutch monarchy from extinction. The grateful couple insisted that the American benefactor become one of the five godparents of little Princess Beatrix. And so Allene, the girl from the livery stables, sat in the front row along with Europe's nobility at the baptism on May 12, 1938.

She sat there bored to tears—as film footage of the hours-long ceremony, held in what was to her unintelligible gibberish, shows. Her face only betrayed signs of pleasure again when, after it was over, she was able to wave to the enthusiastic crowds together with the princely couple.

***

For the Netherlands, still in deep economic crisis, the birth of Princess Beatrix, "bringer of joy," was a welcome glimmer of happiness in dark times. In America, where all the misery had started nine years earlier with the Wall Street Crash of 1929, hope and light were glowing on the horizon. The country had Franklin Roosevelt to thank for this—the Democratic president who, during his inauguration in 1933, declared he would fight the malaise as he would the invasion of a foreign enemy: "I pledge you, I pledge myself, to a new deal for the American people."

The economic recovery program Roosevelt began that year, nick-named the New Deal, was based on the ideas of British economist John Keynes. It consisted of a large number of employment projects, a social safety net for the poorest, pensions for widows and the unemployed, and higher taxes for higher income brackets. Monitoring of banks was tightened, and Prohibition was abolished. As early as 1936, it began to become clear that this program was indeed breathing new life into the beached economy. In November that year, Roosevelt was reelected with the largest majority since the days of the Founding Fathers.

Almost simultaneously, the tide began to turn for the grandiose apartment complex on Park Avenue. John D. Rockefeller Jr., scion of one of the richest families in America, bought the twenty-four-room penthouse. So many buyers followed in his footsteps that the shares the existing owners had been given in exchange for property owner-ship became profitable. Share prices on Wall Street rose again, too, and Allene's fortune—she'd managed to cling to most of her shares—grew in line with it. By 1938, the market was back at full steam, and a news-paper described Allene as one of the wealthiest of American women once again.

In November that year, Allene exchanged her old, relatively small flat in the dark C wing for an eighteen-room apartment in the D wing, the most attractive side of the complex. There she had her own ballroom and a splendid view of both Park Avenue and Seventy-Fifth Street, with light from the southwest. The space and the lovely evening light probably weren't the only reasons for the move. It wasn't inconceivable that she and Paul might have to use their New York address as their main residence and say farewell to their beloved Paris for an indeterminate period of time.

***

By 1938, with his annexation of Austria and part of Czechoslovakia, Adolf Hitler had shown that he wasn't planning to accept the subordinate role the allies had assigned to Germany in Versailles. After a desperate Jewish refugee shot an employee of the German embassy in Paris on November 7, 1938, the German dictator proved to the world that he was serious in his campaign against Jews. During the *Kristallnacht*, the Night of Broken Glass, thousands of Jewish shops were trashed, synagogues were set on fire, and Jewish citizens were abused, humiliated, and murdered.

Many Jewish friends of the Kotzebues, including the Pecci-Blunts, decided not to wait for the inevitable and traveled to New York. Paul and Allene, too, seriously considered returning, an event that, as Paul wrote from Rome to an art-dealer friend in April 1939, "may be sooner than one expects. At any rate we don't feel this is the moment to buy anything."

In a last attempt to stem the aggression flowing from Germany, their phoenixlike traditional enemy, France and England extended a guarantee of independence and mutual assistance to Poland, the state reestablished after the First World War to keep Germany in check on the eastern border. But on August 23, 1939, Hitler made a pact with Joseph Stalin, the Russian dictator who had been in power since the 1920s. Using an iron fist, Stalin had managed to grow the Soviet Union into a global economic power.

Eight days later, in the early morning of September 1, German troops marched on Poland. Several hours later, France and England declared war on Germany. This time there was no trace of the festive eagerness with which Europe had gone to war in 1914—the atrocities of the previous conflagration were too fresh in the memory for this. The winter of 1939–1940 was known as the Phony War, a term invented by American newspapers for that strange time, fraught with anxiety, during which Europe was formally at war but there was no real fighting.

This allowed Allene and Paul to plan their departure from Europe in relative calm. The house on the Rue Barbet-de-Jouy was entrusted to the care of Allene's second cousin, Lucy Tew, who earlier that year had managed to become the second princess in the Tew family, thanks to the mediation of the Kotzebues. She had married one of Russian Prince Dadiani's sons, Georges, like Paul a former member of the czar's court. Apparently Lucy and her husband didn't believe the war would be that bad—or, as in the previous world war, that the Germans wouldn't manage to push on to Paris—since they decided to wait in the French capital for history to take its course.

In November 1939, Paul and Allene left for Rome to clear the apartment on the Piazza d'Aracoeli. In early December, they sailed from Genoa on the SS *Rex*—away from the Old World, with its endless quarrels and feuds, and back to safe, orderly America and their new sun-flooded apartment in New York. A few months later, war did break out in Europe in full force. Beginning with the Netherlands on May 10, 1940, Germany overran half the continent at breakneck speed.

The German advance happened so fast that the Dutch royal family wasn't able to seek refuge at Château de Suisnes, as had been agreed with Allene. Instead, "the Oranjes" fled to England aboard a British Royal Navy destroyer. On June 14, the Germans occupied Paris. England managed to hold its own at first, but the country was ill prepared for war. The Kotzebues had no idea when they would be able to return to their French life, if ever.

***

The Second World War was a remarkably tranquil period in Allene's otherwise stormy life—even if it was only because the war forced her to stay in her own country without interruption for the first time in decades.

Paul, for whom this period of exile was already the third in his life, adapted to life in New York City as well as he could—far from his familiar Paris and his family, who for the most part had stayed there. He allayed his homesickness by becoming the president of the American branch of the Russian Nobility Association and by buying art and antiques, as well as with other pursuits like ballet and the opera. The tall Russian became a familiar sight in the River Café in Central Park, walking distance from 740 Park. He often lunched there with Allene, invariably accompanied by their dogs, a pair of Maltese. For a while they also had a little monkey, but it disappeared without a trace after guests got it drunk on champagne and it bit Allene's hand.

Allene combated her own restlessness and her endless need to be active in her usual manner, namely by buying a house. And what a house it was. In October 1940, she signed a contract for the purchase of Beechwood, the imposing Newport mansion that was once the sanctuary of Mrs. Astor, the unofficial queen of America in Allene's younger years. After her death, it had fallen to her son, John Jacob Astor, who had caused a scandal in 1911 by marrying a classmate of Greta's who was almost thirty years younger than himself. He had died a year later in the shipwreck of the *Titanic*.

Since then, much had changed in and around Newport. Gone were the elegant yachts of the Great White Fleet—instead the bay was now filled with little white sails. Like so many luxury pastimes, sailing had been democratized in the working-class paradise America had transformed itself into. The exorbitant mansions the money-drunk heiresses of the Gilded Age had built were now largely abandoned, and many had been demolished. The housing market's final blow had come from

a large hurricane that had hit Rhode Island and surrounding areas in
September 1938, taking hundreds of lives.

Allene bought the house and its park, in total more than twenty-
two acres, from one of Mrs. Astor's grandsons for the sum of $49,500.
For this bargain price, she could now waltz around the mirrored ballroom in which the high priestess of New York society had once held her
famous summer balls—and where, as a young Mrs. Hostetter, Allene
hadn't been able to get a foothold, as much as she tried.

But more important still was the fact that Beechwood, as one of the
oldest country houses in Newport, was also in one of the best locations,
with a wide view of the ocean both from the house and the park. Now
that she could no longer turn to the comfort of transatlantic crossings,
Allene could at least enjoy the straight line of the horizon from her own
sitting room, something that had always afforded her peace and a sense
of well-being, and fall asleep to the sound of the waves. She had bought
her first seaside house when she was sixty-eight—and now she would
never want anything else.

***

As in the previous world war, the United States tried to stay out of the
conflict that had ignited in Europe. And again, the country found itself
involved nevertheless. With the Japanese attack on Pearl Harbor on
December 7, 1941, America joined the Second World War.

That same month, Allene organized a party at Beechwood on a scale
that hadn't been seen in Newport for years. It included a fashion show,
a dog show, pony races, and a children's carnival to raise money for the
local branch of the Red Cross. In a New York that was ringing with
patriotism as in the old days, she worked on numerous charity events
behind the blackout curtains in her apartment at 740 Park.

Behind the scenes, the Kotzebues had a lot of contact with Juliana,
who now was living in Canada with her three children while Bernhard

remained in London with Queen Wilhelmina. They sponsored a "Blankets for Holland" fundraiser, which was held in the ballroom of the Ritz-Carlton in New York in April 1944. It was also Allene who ensured, via her extensive network, that Bernhard's mother and brother, who had remained in Germany, had sufficient funds and uncensored mail.

During the winter of 1942–1943, the tables turned in the war. After Hitler suddenly turned on the Soviet Union, the German advance was stalled by the tenacious Russian resistance at Stalingrad. The Germans lost in North Africa, too, and in June 1944, the Allies began a massive invasion of Europe from England. On August 25 that year, Paris was freed after four years of occupation. But it was still too early for Allene and Paul to pack their bags again. Just as in the previous world war, the Germans did not concede easily, and it wasn't until spring 1945, following Hitler's suicide, that Germany finally surrendered.

For Bernhard, who, thanks to Wilhelmina, had been promoted to commander of the resistance groups in the occupied Netherlands after the invasion, the delay was a blessing. The Allied command had turned a blind eye to the promotion of the future prince consort, who was completely inexperienced in military matters, because the war seemed practically at an end at that point. But because the war lasted longer than expected, Allene's protégé was able to expand his new role, wielding more power than he could have dreamed of in his future role as prince consort. At the same time, it also brought him lifelong fame as a war hero.

There was another commander in this war with whom Allene shared some history, and this was Robert Greim, the pilot who had shot down her son Teddy's plane in September 1918. Greim had become one of Hitler's most faithful adherents, and after Hermann Göring fell out of grace in April 1945, he took over his role as commander in chief of the Luftwaffe. Just a few days after his promotion, he fell into the hands of the Allies. Fearful of being delivered to the Russians, he ended his life in late May 1945 by swallowing a poison pill.

11

Oceans of Love

Blue—that was the color of Allene's old age, just as green had been the color of her youth. The deep blue of the sea in this period increasingly becoming the leitmotif of her life. The bleached blue of the fabrics she used to decorate her houses. And the practical blue of the sheets of air-mail paper that she covered, one after the other, with her still-elegant handwriting or filled with type using the mini Hermes portable typewriter she took everywhere with her.

Organized as she was, Allene had letterhead stationery printed for each house, from the Rue Barbet-de-Jouy to Park Avenue to Beechwood. Since her divorce from Henry, she often used paper with just a stylized *A* with a crown above it. Officially she had lost her royal status, but in her eyes she was still a princess—an American princess.

During the postwar years, Allene's letters were mainly directed to another legacy of her marriage to Henry: her stepson, whom she'd come to consider even more her own as time passed. In 1918, Allene hadn't been able to save Teddy from the grasping claws of world history, but in 1945, she was given a second chance with Heiner. And she made full use of it, despite her age—she turned seventy-three that year.

Heiner had still been living at Trebschen with his father at the outbreak of the Second World War, but in 1941, when this last remnant of the Reuss estate had to be sold due to lack of funds, he moved into his sister's house in Berlin. Marlisa was newly married to a Berlin businessman who was not of noble birth, and she was mother to a baby daughter. The following year, their father died. Marlisa's husband disappeared from the scene, and the brother and sister spent the rest of the war together with the child, moving to ever-shabbier abodes, driven on by the Allied bombings systematically reducing the German capital to ashes.

Heiner's war efforts remained limited to some translation work for the Wehrmacht. In addition to the perception that he was both physically and psychologically unfit for active service, he benefited from his title for once in his life: from 1940 onward, members of deposed royal houses were banned from joining the Wehrmacht.

Heiner managed to stay under the radar even after the fall of Berlin in the spring of 1945. Like almost all adult men left in the German capital, he was interned for a while, but his interrogators soon realized that there wasn't a rabid Nazi or a war criminal concealed inside this slender, feminine young man and let him go again.

But Heiner was not allowed to leave occupied Berlin—that right was restricted to those who could prove they were victims of Nazi terror. For him and his sister, there was nothing to do but try to survive in the ruined, starving city without any money, without profession or useful contacts, and with their former stepmother as their only lifeline. Allene was saving her own clothing coupons far away in America so that she could provide Heiner with shoes and clothes and did everything she could to get him out of Germany. She ignored Marlisa, who had insulted and hurt her so badly before the war. Allene had washed her hands of Marlisa for good.

Allene hired an expensive Swiss law firm for Heiner and used all her government contacts to get "her son," as she called him, to America.

Every two or three days she wrote him letters, invariably flooded with maternal care and love: "I miss you all the time and find myself constantly turning to speak to you." She ended most of her letters with "Best love to you ever" or her favorite—in the eyes of the reserved Europeans, she remained a rather overemotional American—"Oceans of love, Mama."

***

At first, Allene's quest appeared hopeless. Heiner was a German citizen, and there were few humanitarian reasons he could use to justify preferential treatment. In her words, it was "a struggle with a heavy black cloud, could not get hold of anything." In the meantime, relationships between the former Allies were quickly deteriorating. The chance that the Russians would try to get their hands on Berlin, which was in the middle of the portion of defeated Germany they had been assigned, grew by the day. This meant Heiner's princely title was becoming a real risk for him. The Russians were known for their cruel treatment of anyone who had even the slightest whiff of aristocracy, and two of Heiner's family members who had the misfortune to end up in the Russian occupation zone had not survived their stays in one of the infamous Soviet prison camps.

As usual, Allene wouldn't think of giving up. In the summer of 1947, she managed to acquire departure papers for Heiner on the grounds of a completely fictional story that said he wouldn't be able to withstand the horrors he would have to contend with in both German and Russian captivity. She arranged accommodation for him with a friend in Lausanne, Switzerland, and from New York instructed him like an experienced diplomat about what he should do when he arrived in America:

Be very polite, but use all the arguments you can. Say that
in Washington they told your mother that once you got
out of Germany, they could and would do something. Say
I am a big tax payer and will guarantee your financial position there. Use these same words . . . TELL them you were
put in a German prison as Anti-Nazi and that you have
suffered horrors with the Soviets. Be patient, be polite, but
insist on help. Make as strong a case as possible for yourself
and say as little as possible about the German efforts to
have you back.

While Allene moved heaven and earth in New York that winter
to arrange Heiner's visa and traveled several times to Washington for
it despite the severe weather, Heiner didn't seem to be in any hurry
to reach America. He was enjoying his freedom and the exceptionally comfortable—certainly compared to the poverty he'd suffered in
Berlin—house of Allene's Swiss friend. Even after his stepmother had
managed to secure his visa, he continued to delay his departure. "It is
not necessary at all to wait for the biggest luxury liner," she wrote with
unusual cattiness. "You are a bit spoiled!"

But Allene forgot all her efforts and irritations when she was able
to embrace her prodigal son on the docks of New York in March 1948,
after almost nine years of separation. She put him up at Beechwood,
where he hoped to find a job and build an independent life, an article
in the local newspaper informed its readers. After a while, she returned
to Europe herself, to Paul and their French life, which they soon picked
up again even though their houses had been damaged and partly plundered during the war.

It turned out that Heiner's "escape" from Berlin that Allene had
orchestrated had indeed been just in time. Several months after Heiner's
departure, the Russians blocked all access to the German city's western
part, which was occupied by the British, French, and American forces.

This rang in the start of the Cold War, which would divide the world for decades into a communist power bloc on one hand and a capitalist power bloc on the other. For a while it seemed as if a new world war might break out at any moment, and American expats left Paris en masse to seek a safe haven in their own country. This time, Paul and Allene weren't among those departing. In July 1948, Allene wrote to Heiner in her characteristic staccato style that she didn't think that the Russians wanted a war: "Do not feel the Russians want war, they will get all possible too without." But she also wrote: "How lucky you got out when you did."

***

You often hear about people with a happy childhood, but you seldom hear about people with a happy old age. And yet Allene had this, particularly in the years after she turned seventy-five—officially seventy-one, since she never regained the four years she'd deducted from her age almost twenty years earlier. Just as she'd often trodden unconsciously in the footsteps of her compatriot Edith Wharton before, she did this again with respect to the last phase of her life, which according to the writer certainly had its own charms:

> The farther I have penetrated into this ill-famed Valley, the more full of interest, and beauty too, have I found it. It is full of its own quiet radiance, and in that light I discover many enchanting details which the midday dazzle obscured. As long as I love books and flowers and travel— and my friends—and good food, as I do now, I want no allowances made for me!

A fervent reader Allene was not, but she certainly loved flowers. Her gardens in Suisnes were featured in France's leading gardening magazines, and in Newport she won first prize in the annual flower show for her fuchsias in 1949. And in France, when lilies of the valley were sold everywhere on May Day, she was genuinely upset about the unthinking manner in which the woods were robbed of their wildflowers. "It made me so sad, thousands torn up by the roots, the forests will be denuded soon, so thoughtless and cruel."

Allene fully enjoyed her houses, particularly the one in Suisnes. "Each day I grow to appreciate my lovely home here more, and I am grateful for the years I have enjoyed it . . ." She looked forward to every planned boat trip—"I will enjoy the rest on the boat"—and she liked to write about food, such as "the spaghetti I like so much." As far as her health went, she had little to complain about aside from some rheumatism and, in the words of a Newport admirer, was a "very vibrant woman."

In fact, Allene's only concession to her age was the fact that she released herself from the self-imposed obligation to stay slim at any cost:

> The new man Dior is marvelous, but mostly for young, very slender people. I am too fat for the new models but will have to have them made as well as possible to suit me.

The American economy, stoked by the war, was experiencing yet another period of growth, and Allene had enough money not to have to worry about it. She had enough houses never to feel bored anywhere and enough cars to be able to come and go as she pleased. Her fleet in France alone included a Lincoln Continental, a Chrysler, a Buick, and a Rolls-Royce Silver Wraith, which she had shipped over from Newport. And she had the warm and comforting company of her dogs. During those years she was inseparable from "Mademoiselle Zaza," a Maltese that afforded her a childish kind of pleasure. Without exception, the animal traveled to New York every fall with a new trousseau—an outfit purchased in Paris, consisting of some kind of little sweater and a harness with her name on it.

But most of all, Allene enjoyed the company of other people. Later, a family chronicler of the Kotzebues would describe Paul and Allene's marriage as "a very social life, entertaining and being lavishly entertained." The Château de Suisnes's guest book, which Allene had brought into use in May 1932 with Henry—the first official guest had been the famous Nazi prince Stephan zu Schaumburg-Lippe—was dusted off after the war. In the years since then, the book, bound in heavy black Moroccan leather and inscribed with golden crowns, was filled with pages and pages containing the signatures of the most powerful, rich, frivolous, and amusing people on earth.

Among the many great names to enjoy the Kotzebues' hospitality were famous journalists and writers such as Walter Lippmann and W. Somerset Maugham, as well as leading American politicians like Ambassador Jefferson Caffery; his successor, David Bruce; Warren Austin, a United Nations representative, and future Secretary of State John Foster Dulles. George Marshall, the father of the Marshall Plan— an American aid initiative to help prevent Europe from sliding toward communism—was a regular visitor to Suisnes. British Prime Minister Winston Churchill, so greatly admired by Allene, was also part of their extended circle of colorful acquaintances. "Saw him at the station when I went for Olive, he looked happy and gay," she once wrote.

Allene had tea in Versailles with the former commander-in-chief of the Allied forces and later president Dwight Eisenhower. Her dance card was filled with all kinds of (deposed) royalty, such as the former king of Italy, the Norwegian crown prince, Prince Paul of Yugoslavia, Princess Kira of Prussia, and Princess Ghislaine, the widow of the prince of Morocco. "Regular" Americans were often behind the grand titles in the guest book. Princess Emily Cito-Filomarino di Bitetto had been the all-American-sounding Emily Taylor before her marriage to an Italian prince, and the elderly but irrepressible Baroness Bateman of Shobdon had come into the world in New York as Marion Graham.

An unusual case was Allene's friend Valerie, Duchess von Arenberg. She had grown up as a commoner, adopted by Jewish foster parents in Hungary, and her real father, Duke von Schleswig-Holstein, only recognized her as his lawful daughter on his deathbed. That recognition rendered her one of Queen Victoria's great-grandchildren.

In fact, Allene seemed to have just one real requirement of her companions, and that was that they were entertaining. In this respect, the Duke of Windsor—former British king Edward VIII, who had given up the throne in 1936 to marry American divorcée Wallis Simpson—committed a mortal sin in her eyes:

> Went last night to the American Embassy to dine, 22 at table for the Duke and Duchess of Windsor. She so tiny but lovely figure and white silk dress, tight. No jewels except sapphire ring, white earrings and tiny black cape of many little black lace ruffles. I sat next to him and think him a bore.

When a dinner was not entertaining enough for Allene's tastes, she would jolly it up herself, as her friend George Post Wheeler later recalled:

> My friend of other years, Allene Burchard, later Princess Henry 33rd of Reuss and at present Countess Kotzebue, was lunching at the Dutch Legation in Paris (she being godmother, with the Countess of Athlone, to Queen Juliana's oldest daughter) and was seated next to King Gustav. He carried a cigarette box mounted with topazes and set it on the table beside his plate. It happened that Allene had one almost exactly like it in size and mounting,

and when he was looking the other way she laid hers close beside him. When he turned and saw the two he started violently, put his hand to his forehead, and exclaimed in a scared voice: But this is not possible! It's getting me, I'm seeing double!

***

After many years, the ice had even been broken between Allene and the old Dutch queen, who had withdrawn almost entirely from the public eye by then. "No one could work harder for [her] country than Queen Wilhelmina," Allene wrote. Aside from this, Allene was particularly fond of Bernhard's younger brother, Aschwin, for whom she'd arranged a work permit and a job as a Far Eastern art specialist in New York's Metropolitan Museum of Art. In recognition of her efforts, Wilhelmina would later bestow on her the title of Honorary Lady to the House of Orange—"which I thought most kind of her," according to the lady in question.

Naturally Allene was also an honorary guest at Juliana's inauguration on September 6, 1948, in Amsterdam. She gave Heiner an extensive and opinionated account. Bernhard, she wrote with almost maternal pride, was "a perfect show" in his admiral's uniform, while Juliana garnered her approval by having lost a lot of weight for the occasion:

> She is so THIN now and truly looks lovely and such jewels . . . her hair well done, the crowd went wild with excitement. All too beautiful and perfectly done . . . Everyone is extremely nice to me and I was given same rank and courtesy and attention as the Royalties here and they were very charming as well.

If one thing is clear from Allene's letters that have been preserved, it is that as an old woman, she was still essentially the same excitable girl from Jamestown, looking at the world and people around her with an open mind, full of curiosity. At the same time she took pleasure in the simple things of life, like a vacation with Paul and with Alice Brown, her secretary-cum-lady-companion and friend, in a "tiny lovely house in the woods" in New Hampshire. "I do the cooking, Miss Brown the garden and Paul the wood." Or in an evening in, with just Alice for company. "When we're alone, we dine in the little round salon, it's so cozy and peaceful, I like it so much when she reads and I write."

Perhaps this was Allene's greatest achievement, above her wealth, her titles, her many houses, and her impressive guest book: that despite everything she'd experienced and endured, she always clung to her ability to enjoy life and be grateful for it.

***

Allene had been and remained the Queen of Loose Ends. Every time a hole developed in the fabric of her life, she'd tie together the loose ends and get on with it. Her past was useful for this—other people may have spent more and more time immersed in their memories as they aged, but Allene kept the cabinet of her personal history firmly locked. In this respect, she proved herself a child of Victorian times. She had no need for modern ideas about mourning or the expression of feelings. Her philosophy was to keep going and not look back.

It was the attitude that had made America great, it was the mentality that allowed Allene to survive, and it was also the spirit that she tried to instill in her stepson, who made little effort in Newport to build himself an independent life:

> Strength of character has to be worked on, hard . . . Always
> try many things. Try every way one can think of, when you
> truly need something important and if you do not see the

way, get help . . . All girls and boys, no matter what position they have should be brought up to work these days, or at least know how to. I should think every effort should be to get work for your own dignity . . .

TRY to make friends, everyone can with an effort. Everyone has sadness and much trouble and likes a gay pleasant friend about. COURAGE ALL THE TIME.

Heiner's part of the correspondence has not survived, but from Allene's reactions, the contents can be guessed at. Above all else, he felt himself to be a victim of his times, of circumstance, and of other people. The fact that he never managed to find work or friends or have a relationship but continued to camp out in Beechwood, cared for by Allene's servants, was never down to him but always to others, who had fallen short in his eyes in some way or other.

Allene tried in vain to convince him that being hard on yourself didn't mean you had to be hard on others. On the contrary, she told him:

It is thoroughly stupid to harbor resentments to anyone, I WILL NOT DO IT, it would hurt me more than the other person . . . You MUST, MUST not always think the worst. I could take offense daily with people but personally think it stupid not to have a friendly feeling to all. It is a better character disposition in life . . . show tolerance.

I like people and you MUST, also it is true that we get from people very MUCH WHAT WE GIVE THEM. Look for their good qualities and ignore their faults, that way one is happier [. . .] Take people as they are, know yourself [. . .] If we took people for their true count, we would have few friends.

Allene practiced her own recipe for happiness with verve. Indeed, she seemed not to want or be able to see certain things taking place around her. Like the fact that, despite all her assistance and urgings, Heiner kept putting off any plans for a career or marriage indefinitely, preferring the company of young men with a "dubious reputation" in terms of their sexual preferences. Or the fact that her own husband, Paul, often went out with his much younger nephew George, who went through life with the cheerful nickname of "Gogo."

In this sense, Allene may have had a pseudo husband in Paul, just as she had a pseudo son in Heiner and pseudo daughters in Kitty Cohu and Jane Moinson. But she saw that as no reason to love them any less unconditionally than if they'd been genuine. Just as the amputees from the First World War had learned to live with artificial limbs and even become used to them, Allene made do with an artificial family. There was no space in her philosophy of life for wasting time contemplating lost loves or becoming a captive of her own past.

***

Allene preferred to look ahead—as in the summer of 1951, when, approaching eighty, she bought a house on the coast "in a whim," as she wrote. She had gone to the south coast of France to visit her old friend Marion Bateman in Monte Carlo and, once there, had fallen back in love with the Riviera. "It's so lovely here, all the roses out now and the perfume of flowers everywhere." On the way, she visited a summerhouse that Kitty and Wally Cohu had rented earlier. It was in Cap d'Ail, a village between Nice and Monaco. She decided to make an offer on it at once. In early July she wrote to Heiner:

> Have been very foolish and extravagant, as cannot afford it, but have bought a tiny villa at Cap d'Ail, about twenty minutes' walk from Monte Carlo, right on the sea. No

furniture in it, but if you like could get three beds and six chairs and a bridge table and picnic there within a week. And I do the cooking and we all wash dishes, and we can swim off the place. Let me know if you would like this!

Until the end of the nineteenth century, Cap d'Ail had been a farming village built into a steep, rocky mountainside, visited only by goatherds. But the construction of a railway between Nice and Monaco had transformed the village into a hot spot for the international jet set, including the British royal family and Winston Churchill, who liked to set up his easel and paint in the famous Hotel Eden. It was also popular as a winter resort since the Maritime Alps formed a natural barrier against the cold winds from the north. It was the ultimate place to enjoy *la douceur de vivre*—the gentle life.

Castel Mare, as Allene's new house was called, was not big, but it was wonderfully situated—right on the seafront, at the end of the Boulevard de Mer. A small pebbled beach could be reached via a flight of stairs with the poetic name l'Escalier de la Solitude—the steps of solitude. The summerhouse was built in 1909 for a rich manufacturer from Monaco and was so tightly nestled into the rock face that you could see its roof from the boulevard. It was the ultimate seaside house, with an uninterrupted view of the Mediterranean Sea on three sides. On the shallow terrace at the front of the house you might almost imagine yourself aboard a ship, there was so much splashing foam and so omnipresent was the sound of the waves constantly pounding the rocks below.

A month after Allene had signed the purchase agreement, in August 1951, she organized her first little dinner "just in a picnic fashion." In the months that followed, she busied herself with setting up her new Mediterranean life. The Buick was replaced by a Ford Vedette because it was much more practical for the narrow, winding roads. The house was equipped with a telephone connection, modernized, and redecorated.

Allene had furniture sent over from both Paris and New York and bought the rest of her furnishings at the Parisian department store Galeries Lafayette and other exclusive stores.

The house's pièce de résistance, and the part Allene paid the most attention to, was the room the workmen respectfully termed "la Chambre de Madame." She decorated her bedroom—which took up more than half of the first floor and had large, high windows on two sides and doors opening onto a balcony—with the finest satins and the softest silks in delicate shades of blue—almost as though she wanted the room to dissolve into the azure sea, of which she had such a magnificent view from her bed.

12

How not to Die

The last act of the play in which Allene had the leading role began in Newport's court of law on a lovely spring morning in 1955, some weeks after her death. Two years earlier, Heiner Reuss had sworn an oath of allegiance to the American flag in this rather pompous building dating from the Gilded Age and had become a naturalized American citizen. And now he was here again—but this time as a man who was publicly being made out to be somebody who had cheated money out of the dying elderly stepmother for whose care he was responsible. The amount in question was an impressive $23.6 million. The court case was the largest ever to take place in Newport. "A live court room drama such as no summer theater could hope to offer," the *Chicago Daily Tribune* promised its readers.

And a drama it was, if only because of the unclear family relation-ships at the root of the conflict. The plaintiffs were a group of a dozen or so of Allene's nephews and nieces, coming from all four corners of America: New York, San Francisco, Berkeley, Miami, and Palm Beach. Among them was Lucy Dadiani, the young niece whose marriage to a Russian prince Allene had once arranged but with whom Allene had quarreled when she found the house she'd left in the Dadianis' care plundered when she returned to it in the summer of 1945. Allene had written to Heiner, disillusioned:

> Lucy stole all the good things that were at Barbet-de-Jouy.
> I trusted her and Georges and they turned out to be only
> thieves. I fear both will go to jail. I have no sympathy for
> them, they betrayed all my trust.

Allene never did take them to court, since it became clear that the Dadianis hadn't so much stolen the things themselves as allowed German occupiers to. But the matter had been covered extensively in the international press and hadn't helped the already cool relations between Allene and her biological family grow any warmer.

Another famous name in the Tew camp was Julia Rosewater, the young relative with whom Allene had been so close in the years around Anson's death. Their relationship had been so close that in 1928, Julia had even gone so far as to have her then-seventeen-year-old son Seth's name officially changed to Burchard. In doing so, his mother, according to an article in the *New York Times* titled "Took Burchard Name, Inherits Millions," believed that he would not only have a right to Anson's millions but also, in due course, to Allene's. Clearly Julia had jumped the gun a bit, because although Allene financed Seth's, or "Burchard's," Harvard education and later helped him find work at General Electric, he wasn't named at all in her will.

***

On the first day of the trial, May 22, 1955, the "heirs at law and next of kin" provided a list of ten arguments why the document purported to be Allene's last will and testament should be declared invalid. To summarize,

[T]he will was made as a result of undue, illegal and improper influence, and as a result of duress, the testator was not of sound mind and sufficient mental capacity, the instrument was not the last will, and was not executed with all formalities required by law.

In a nutshell, Allene's family wanted to have her declared insane retroactively.

It didn't seem that this would prove much of an obstacle to the Tews. The contents and the circumstances surrounding the creation of Countess Kotzebue's will were suspicious, to say the least. In their eyes, it was remarkable that she would leave the lion's share of her fortune to what a journalist later described as "a retinue of servants and hangers-on," in particular the men who'd functioned as her son and her husband in the last years of her life. Not only were both gentlemen of "dubious sexual orientation," they had backgrounds that, in those years of the Cold War and witch-hunting of Communists, made alarm bells ring.

Heiner Reuss was German born and, naturalized or not, after two world wars could only be seen by those with prejudices as a long-established enemy of the United States. Paul Kotzebue, no less than twelve years younger than his deceased wife and suspect enough for this reason, was actually a Russian and, in this, the embodiment of the new enemy. There were even questionable aspects to Kitty Cohu, the third-largest beneficiary in the will. She was certainly American, but she was also married to the lawyer who had drawn up the contested will and who was now acting as its executor. To make the conflict of interest even greater, it turned out that the deceased had been a silent partner in Wally Cohu's legal firm, albeit not under her own name but as A. T. Burchard.

The most suspicious thing of all was the course of events surrounding Allene's death. Why, the nieces and nephews asked, hadn't their terminally ill aunt returned to New York the previous fall, as was her custom? She would have been able to await the end in her comfortable apartment on Park Avenue with America's best doctors and hospitals at her fingertips rather than having to die in a kind of summerhouse on the coast, assisted solely by an old French doctor in his eighties. Why hadn't she wanted to see anyone anymore, far away in France—not even the family members with whom she was still on good terms? And why had she been buried immediately after her death in that foreign country, in complete silence, so that no one had been able to say goodbye to her?

This was what the Newport Court had to determine: What had actually happened to Allene Tew during those last years?

***

The symptoms had actually begun in the fall of 1951, just after she'd bought the villa at Cap d'Ail. Allene had been suffering from stomach complaints for a while and had had an unusual lack of appetite, certainly for her. "Zaza is gobbling up her dinner here beside me in the boudoir," she said in a letter to Heiner, "wish I had some of hers and Paul's appetite."

In October, the pain became so severe that after returning home from a canasta evening at a friend's house in Paris, she didn't even manage to finish her weekly letter to Heiner. The assistance of Dr. Louis Moinson—the father of the French girl whose marriage Allene had once arranged at Birchwood and whom she'd always watched over with maternal care—was called for. The famous Paris surgeon, in his advanced age, had retired, but he still served as a personal physician to friends and family.

"I think she was fighting it for a long time & hope after Dr. M.'s treatment she will be better," Alice Brown wrote later that evening to Heiner in Allene's place. Four days later, Allene did indeed feel better and was already feeling chatty again, as her next letter to Heiner reveals:

I know it was a liver attack, but Dr. wrongly said it was intestinal poisoning and kept me miserable longer than necessary.

The Kotzebues spent that winter in New York, as usual. Allene reigned over the overseas part of her kingdom by letter with her habitual discipline, but she still didn't feel completely fit. "Try to keep cheerful and hope all will last out my life," she wrote to John Burnet, a British war veteran who worked as her handyman in France and was keeping an eye on the refurbishments at Cap d'Ail.

Nothing came of her plans to journey to the Riviera in March to admire the results of the renovations. Instead, she ended up in New York's Roosevelt Hospital, where a malignant tumor was removed from her stomach. It appears the doctors didn't give Allene much hope of recovery, because on Monday, April 7, 1952, still in the hospital and in the company of Wally Cohu, she drew up her will. She endorsed the document with a signature that was as firm and self-assured as when she'd first signed herself "Allene Tew Hostetter" at age nineteen.

A few days later, Allene put Beechwood up for sale. As earlier correspondence showed, she hadn't felt at home for years in the mausoleum-like country house that had once belonged to Mrs. Astor. It really only served as a place for Heiner to live—Heiner, who four years after his arrival in America still hadn't been able to find work or accommodation of his own.

It wasn't very difficult to find a buyer for the legendary Astor mansion in Newport in this time of economic prosperity, and on May 3, the house, including much of its contents, was sold to a New York yarn manufacturer. Allene had smaller pieces of furniture shipped to France to further furnish Castel Mare; the crockery and textiles were shared out among friends and acquaintances such as Bernhard's brother: "China and glass given to Prince Lippe."

But Allene hadn't had her fill of the view of the sea or Rhode Island's bay. As soon as she was released from the hospital, she rented a house on the farthest tip of the Newport peninsula, surround on three sides by the Atlantic Ocean. Again she was following in Edith Wharton's footsteps—the writer had lived at precisely this spot for years, before her departure to Paris—seduced by "the endlessly changing moods of the misty Atlantic" and "the night-long sound of the surges against the cliffs."

In 1927, the famous architect John Russell Pope built a summerhouse for himself and his family near Edith Wharton's former home Land's End. The Waves, as the result was befittingly named, was surrounded by rocks overgrown with wild roses and polished by the ocean, so typical to Rhode Island's bay. Just as in Cap d'Ail, the sound of the sea and the smell of seaweed were everywhere, but here the atmosphere was more peaceful, with swallows nesting in the stone walls around the garden.

At the back of her new living quarters, Allene had a view of Bailey's Beach, where, in 1953, Jacqueline Bouvier, one of her neighbors at 740 Park, celebrated her engagement to the young, very promising senator John F. Kennedy. At the front, she had a seascape that stretched out all the way to Ireland.

***

"Trust you are quite yourself again," wrote Allene's Cap d'Ail handyman, John Burnet, in June 1952 to his employer, whom he was clearly very fond of. Allene was indeed more or less herself—in any case, enough of herself to take the boat to Europe the following month and to resume her life as a wealthy nomad. That summer she lunched with W. Somerset Maugham, had drinks with one of Churchill's daughters, and was given a new puppy to replace Mademoiselle Zaza, who had died and was sorely missed. She and Paul also bought a television set, the new invention that was taking over the world at high speed and that played a major role in the election victory of Allene's friend "Ike" Eisenhower later that year.

In September, Allene hosted the Dutch royal family for a short vacation in Cap d'Ail. Juliana had, coincidentally, just arrived in New York for her first American state visit when Allene had surgery there in April. The queen had immediately made space in her busy schedule for what the Dutch newspapers discreetly called "a visit to an old, ailing friend." Bernhard did not accompany her, even though he was in New York at that point, too. The relationship between the queen and prince consort had been strained for years due to his extramarital escapades and Juliana's deepening friendship with the faith healer Greet Hofmans. During this state visit, the relationship sank to a new low point when Juliana made a pacifist speech at Congress, expressly against Bernhard's wishes.

It seems that Allene did what she could to bring the estranged couple back together again, since she spent a remarkable amount of time with them that fall. After their vacation, she had lunch with them at the embassy in Paris several times; she also had Bernhard and his two eldest daughters to stay a few times separately. This delighted her four-teen-year-old goddaughter, Beatrix, who, like her father, was unusually attached to the decisive American, so different from her often-doubting and passive mother.

The attempts at reconciliation didn't amount to much—the discord in the marriage would lead to a publicly fought royal battle shortly after Allene's death. It was, as an American paper remarked during that period, a pity that Countess Kotzebue was no longer there "to mediate or offer Bernhard sage advice." Allene herself spoke pithily of marital crises like the Oranjes' in a letter to Heiner: "It is so tiresome that people are not kinder to each other."

***

"Don't play any more tricks like last year," wrote John Burnet to Allene in the spring of 1953. He got his way, because that year his employer did return to Cap d'Ail in March after her winter in New York to see how things were going with her impulse purchase of two years earlier. She carried her complete set of New York silverware in her luggage because "picnic fashion" or not, she liked to dine in style. She wrote enthusiastically to Heiner:

> Weather, sea, sky and flowers: all wonderful and I do appreciate being here [. . .] IT IS VERY RESTFUL and doing me good.

For her health, she could consult Dr. Moinson, who lived with his wife in nearby Monte Carlo. He provided her with more than enough pain-killing pills and injections and came by almost every day to check on her:

> He feels if he watches constantly my blood count, pressure and general condition he can get me strong and well. I know his heart is in it & hope he is right.

But in the meantime, the guest list for Allene's upcoming birthday celebration in Suisnes, an event she'd had so much pleasure organizing the previous year and had celebrated so exuberantly, grew shorter and shorter. Her social diary became emptier, too. She often opted for a "little supper with Miss Brown" and then went to bed early—only, the next day, to hide in her seasoned, hardy manner the fact that she'd been in too much pain to sleep: "The moon is again too beautiful over the sea, I watched it quite a while in the night." Traveling was also becoming more difficult:

The trip up [to Paris] tired me far too much, could hardly move for 48 hours, now have taken the strongest pill and will surely be better soon.

As Louis Moinson prescribed stronger and stronger painkillers over the course of 1953 and 1954, the life Allene had always liked to keep so free and spacious slowly shriveled. But the way she'd always refused to let the ghosts of her past into her life was also the way she behaved toward death, the other shadow creeping ever closer.

***

Allene's homemade recipe for happiness in life had always worked well. Again and again, she'd confronted adversity and despair with her favorite mantras. "If one has the will and persistence, one CAN do things . . . always try every possible way, and if you don't see a way, ask for help . . . COURAGE ALL THE TIME." And each time she had managed to turn the course of events her way, force fate's hand, and find a new form of happiness.

But this philosophy didn't work in the face of her new enemy. The illness that was eating away at Allene from the inside could not be banished with all the willpower and persistence in the world, and denying it only backfired.

How not to die? This question began to dominate Allene's thoughts more and more as the year 1954 progressed. And because she'd learned never to give up hope, she reached for ever more unorthodox treatment methods—and in so doing lost what had always been her strength, in combination with her courage: her common sense. At the beginning of the summer, she wrote hopefully to Heiner of "cures in England without a medicine [. . .] sounds foolish but Hope has known some marvelous results, so why not try?"

In July, she visited two German "miracle" doctors in Montreux, Switzerland, who had promised to heal her with ferrous serums containing placenta cells. As her letters show, initially Allene trusted blindly in her new therapists and their treatment: "Have taken two doses of Dr. Niehans's cells and he thinks I takes them very well"—although it didn't escape her still-sharp mind that both gentlemen were raking in a fortune with their revolutionary treatments:

> All this very expensive but if it cures worthwhile [. . .] I feel like guinea pig with all sorts of [stitches], medicines, etc. but Dr. Niehans feels some can help.

Six weeks later, there was not a single improvement in Allene's condition, reason for Niehans's colleague to make her life as their patient real hell now:

> Dr. Ackermann took away all cigarettes and all medicine . . . very strict diet . . . too miserable to write, more soon.

After this, the letters with which Allene kept her stepson in America updated on her ups and downs became shorter, the handwriting ever jerkier. "Had serum from second placenta . . . still suffer plenty," she wrote on August 30. Six days later the letter followed that would be her last to Heiner: "Bad day for me but much love. When do you think you can leave?"

Shortly after this, Allene, by now completely exhausted, traveled back to her summerhouse on the Riviera, the closest of all of her houses. She'd lost her last wager with life—traveling on to New York or even Paris was not even thinkable. And so her odyssey finally ran aground in the fall of 1954 on the rocks of Cap d'Ail. The only thing she could do was wait for the winter and the inevitable in her Blue Room, surrounded by her self-selected family, and try to find an answer for her final challenge: How to die?

***

On July 12, 1955, less than six weeks after the start of "Case 9400"— as the suit the Tews had launched against the heirs was called—the court in Newport came to the conclusion that Allene's testament met all the requirements of legality and could therefore be considered legitimate. The results of the hearings with the nursing staff from Roosevelt Hospital were completely clear: Allene Kotzebue had been completely compos mentis when she'd signed her will in April 1952, and there had been no question of "undue influence."

Yet it would be another eight years before the file was finally closed and the inheritance could be shared out definitively. The long judicial process could not be based on the strength of the claims—aside from accusations, the Tew family could raise no concrete incriminating facts or witnesses, and newspapers soon lost interest in the case. It seems more likely it was because of the Cold War, which held America in its grip. As open-minded toward foreigners as Americans had been during Allene's youth, when the country still needed to be built, they proved to be xenophobic and intolerant now, in a period when there was so much wealth to lose.

The process dragged on endlessly—stalled and delayed by the Tews, who might not have stood to gain anything but could at least ensure that the people Allene had left her money to couldn't get at it. They may have realized their case was hopeless from the start, a fact possibly evident in the radical way one of them decided to cut his losses on December 22, 1955. On that day, a cousin of Lucy Dadiani's, forty-two-year-old James Dinsmore Tew Jr., drove onto the tracks of the Florida East Coast Railway and pulled on his hand brake. A few minutes later, his vehicle was snatched by a train and dragged along for a mile and a half. The handwritten note left behind in his inside pocket revealed that this nephew of Allene's had retained a certain sense of decency. "The driver is not to blame," he had written.

James Tew Jr.'s suicide had no effect on the court case: his place in the Tew camp was immediately taken over by his ex-wife, who demanded $150,000 from the legacy for her son and litigated just as hardheadedly as the rest.

***

Paul and Heiner were lucky in one respect: Allene turned out to have already apportioned her French possessions in a separate, undisputed will written in November 1951. In it, she had stated that the house on Rue Barbet-de-Jouy would go to Paul, Heiner would get the villa in Cap d'Ail, and Château de Suisnes would go to Kitty and Wally Cohu.

Paul and Heiner returned to France for good, and Wally sold the apartment on Park Avenue in January 1956; as executor, he'd been given permission by the court to handle any ongoing business. Among the many people interested in Allene's flat was a young actress named Elizabeth Taylor. The cooperative's board turned her down as a potential occupant because of the supposedly frivolous nature of her profession. Instead, the apartment went to a Mr. Walter Chrysler Jr., the heir to the automobile empire of the same name. A few months after he had moved in, the contents were auctioned, including the art collection Allene and Anson had built up together.

In July 1963, Newport's court of law pronounced its final verdict. All of the Tews' claims were refused, and the legacy, which for the most part was made up of shares in American companies and by then had a total value of almost $24 million, could finally be allocated. "Now I am really rich," Paul said to a family member when he returned to Paris after the verdict.

The bulk of Allene's wealth was divided into three parts, according to her final will, each to be put into a trust fund. The proceeds from the first fund went to Paul, and those of the second, to Kitty. The third fund was given in its entirety to the Stevens Institute of Technology in New Jersey on the condition that it be used to set up a department named after Anson Wood Burchard.

Allene's impressive jewelry collection went to a range of friends and female family members. Aside from this, she left dozens of bequests to friends, staff, and other people who, for whatever reason, had a special place in her heart. Her secretary, Alice Brown, who had followed her around the world like a faithful shadow for more than twenty-five years, received the sum of $50,000, which was more than enough for her to go and live off her private means in the Virgin Islands.

Shortly after the verdict, Paul sold the house on the Rue Barbet-de-Jouy. He and his nephew George moved to an apartment in the elegant and discreet Parisian suburb of Neuilly-sur-Seine. Two years later he officially adopted his nephew as a son, making George the heir to both his title and his personal possessions.

Later, another nephew would write that, despite severe diabetes and asthma, Paul remained a proud man right up to the end of his life, "standing upright whatever the circumstances"—just as he'd learned in the Page Corps. Attempts to lure the czar's former guard into revealing details about his past came to nothing. "I have secrets and they'll go with me to my grave," he said.

Paul took his secrets to his grave in September 1966, after he'd been fatally injured in a traffic accident near the northern Italian city of Vercelli while on his way to the Adriatic coast. He was buried next to his mother and his sister in the English cemetery in Nice, a few hundred meters from the place where Allene had been laid to rest in 1955. It was thus a matter of "lying apart together"—in fact, just as they had done during their almost-twenty-year marriage.

***

Heiner, who inherited the proceeds of his designated trust fund after Paul's death, as Allene's will dictated, never became the man his stepmother had tried to make of him. In the days following her death, he sealed off the top floor of Castel Mare, closed all the windows, and shut himself up in his room on the ground floor. There he lived like a hermit, only going out to stock up on coffee and perfume—possibly a reaction to his traumatic war experiences in Berlin—visiting from time to time Morocco's gay capital, Marrakesh. Each year, he had a bouquet of pink and white carnations laid on Allene's grave to mark the anniversary of her death. Heiner died in 1993, seventy-seven years old and practically blind from his heavy smoking. He left Castel Mare to the daughter of his by-then-deceased sister, Marlisa.

And then, decades after Allene's death, it became clear just how clear minded she had been on the day she'd signed her will in Roosevelt Hospital. The trust fund that had gone to Heiner after Paul's death could not be left to his niece, just as Paul had not been able to bequeath his to his "Gogo." Instead, it went to the family of the only family member Allene apparently hadn't felt was after her money: Charlotte Rosewater, Seth's, or "Burchard's," older sister.

Charlotte was a young lady after Allene's own heart: she had studied chemistry, and she was independent and incredibly enterprising. In 1937, in her early thirties at the time and visiting Allene, she had fallen head over heels in love with a British man, who, just like Allene's son, had fought as a pilot in the First World War. The couple had married in Allene's house and moved back to England after a few years, and there Charlotte's husband had played an important role in the British army's information network.

Later, their daughter Anne would still remember vividly her mother and Allene reuniting in the Ritz Hotel in London directly after the war. At the time just ten years old, she formed her own impressions of this

American auntie who had initiated the tea party. "I found her slightly intimidating and rather awe-inspiring: she told my mother I was very weedy, and I was terribly insulted."

Anne could hardly have guessed back then that the formidable old lady would bequeath her parents $200,000. And neither could she have guessed that she and her family—after Kitty's death in 1977 and again in 1993, after Heiner's death—would be buried under a waterfall of dollars from the two trust funds that had turned out to be destined for them.

Allene, unpredictable and strong willed to the end, had left her fortune to somebody for whom money really had no importance when they met: a little girl who was deeply offended because she'd been called "weedy."

EPILOGUE

The Blue Room II

Spring 1955

How to die? Well, the same way a person has lived. And in Allene's case, this meant in style. However difficult that may have been in a drafty, awkward house with lots of stairs. However turbulent it may have been as the sea lost more and more of its summery friendliness and charm with the advance of fall. The shutters of the neighboring houses had closed up one after the other—the winter visitors preferring to tuck themselves away in the comfortable villas and hotels higher in the hills and not down there, right on the seafront, exposed to all the elements.

At first, Allene stubbornly tried to patch up the pieces of her old life. "If one has the will and persistence, one CAN do things." Early in the morning, she went downstairs and woke up her stepson in order to go through the stock prices in the morning papers. She had manicures and pedicures every week so that she stayed, in Heiner's words, "the most elegant in the world," despite the ravages the illness was perpetrating on her insides. She drank pink champagne. And sometimes, on good days, she had herself carried in a wicker deck chair up from the terrace to the boulevard for a trip to Monaco, where she'd entertain herself by gambling and playing card games in a private dining room.

At the same time, she made arrangements for things like her own funeral. She wanted to be buried between her two parents in the English part of La Caucade, with its magnificent view of the sea and, already in those years, the continuous taking off and landing of airplanes. Her grave monument was to be of white marble, with space left open for plants and flowers. Her name would be carved on it: "Countess Allene de Kotzebue, born Tew," with the date of birth she had invented for herself—1876—underneath, and the year of her death. And at the foot of her tomb, the following words would be chiseled: "Widow of Anson Wood Burchard."

For this was something Allene had always known herself: her first two husbands had married her mainly for her looks and the last two mainly for her money; the middle husband was the only one who had genuinely loved her for herself.

***

The year 1955 dawned. In Eastern Europe, preparations were in full swing for the Warsaw Pact, a counterpart to NATO. In the French colonies of Algeria, Morocco, and Tunisia, violent uprisings against the colonial governments broke out. The United States had launched its first nuclear submarine. In Èze, a village close to Cap d'Ail, filming was wrapping up on Alfred Hitchcock's *To Catch a Thief*. The lead roles were played by Cary Grant and Grace Kelly, who a year later would become another American princess, in Monaco.

But Allene cared less and less about such things. Her universe was shrinking to the blue boudoir on the first floor of Castel Mare, where she spent her days in her blue silk bed, drowsing in a haze of morphine and champagne. From time to time, though not very often, she managed to write a letter, usually to offer some final maternal advice to one of her protégés. "Take life as easy as you can," she wrote to Bernhard in January, "health is the best of all gifts." But when he was in the area in early April and wanted to visit her, he wasn't granted access to her sickbed. Allene felt that her humiliation was great enough already.

Outside was a foreign country—foreign in terms of its language and smells, foreign, too, in the rugged, rocky landscape so different from the gentle rolling hills of her youth. Outside was the raging sea, and in the hearth, in which a fire was kept burning day and night, the flames danced as they once had in her grandfather's smithy in Jamestown.

Yet Allene did not die. Perhaps after such a long and eventful life, she needed that whole long winter to think everything over. Perhaps it was the morphine, which Louis Moinson administered in ever larger quantities, that broke open the locks on the closets where she had stowed away her past, causing the memories to come tumbling out.

On the nightstand next to her bed, the photos piled up—Greta in her wedding dress, Teddy in his uniform, herself as a young girl with her cousin, looking into the photographer's lens with her usual impertinence.

Or perhaps Allene had simply resolved to make it through to the spring.

***

The end came on Sunday, May 1, at half past six in the morning. Outside, the mimosa was blossoming, and down below, the white prows of the first wooden speedboats plowed through the blue, now quieted Mediterranean Sea. Young, beautiful people had fun together in Riva motorboats, unaware of their own mortality, of the shutters closed up there above the rocks or the struggle that was taking place behind them. That morning, all the women who had once been inside Allene, like *matryoshka* nesting dolls from Paul's Russian childhood, died, too. The ambitious blond girl from the tough pioneering town and the young mother practicing endlessly with her children on the horse-jumping course beside a large log cabin on the Ohio River, the independent businesswoman from New York's high society, Anson's happy spouse on Long Island, and the American princess with her sad past. And, after that, the countess with the Russian name who became a godmother to royalty and crafted her own form of happiness.

Allene's very last car ride was along the Route du Littoral—the road that snakes along the Mediterranean between Monaco and Nice, often called the most beautiful in the world. Only a few minutes after her body had been carried out and started on its final journey, the doors of the Blue Room were locked—to remain so for forty years.

It wasn't until 1993, when Heiner Reuss died in the self-enforced solitude he'd preferred in life, that keys grated in the lock once more and strange voices sounded throughout the room. The shutters that had rusted were forced open, and for the first time in years, sunlight fell upon Allene's final décor: her clothes, her dressing table at the corner window, the figurines of monkeys and dogs she'd liked to surround herself with, the photos next to the bed, and the bed itself, the blue fabric still covered in bloodstains, witnesses of her final illness. A side table, its top a tiled picture of Suisnes. Letters. Chairs covered in silk that was so rotten it pulverized at the touch. The small Hermes typewriter.

Fresh air streamed into the Blue Room through the high windows and the open balcony doors. The faded curtains swayed in the sea wind. The fabric was blown upward, and with it, all of Allene's dreams, pain, and memories flowed out across the sea and into the wide world.

AUTHOR'S NOTE

It was there in that world that I discovered parts of the marvelous adventures of Allene Tew. My treasure hunt took me to all kinds of places, such as New York City, Paris, Jamestown, Pittsburgh, and Newport; to many libraries and newspaper archives; to all kind of historians and other people I never would have met otherwise.

But it all began on the terrace of Allene's seaside house in Cap d'Ail, which in the summer of 2009—still writing my dissertation on the young Prince Bernhard—I visited for the first time. That very afternoon I thought: *I'm going to write a book about this woman.* The billion-dollar question is why? Why do you decide to dedicate years of your own life to someone you never knew, whom at that moment you know very little about, and of whom you've never even seen a good photograph?

In retrospect, I think that in the first instance, it was mainly a romantic notion. For years I'd had the idea of writing a book about an old woman in a coastal house, looking back over her life. When the current owner of Castel Mare told me that Allene had been forced to spend the last six months of her life in this house, I immediately sensed that I'd found my protagonist. There was also the fact that Allene was an American. After covering mainly Dutch and German history in my previous books, I felt like taking on something bigger, in particular America.

The latter had to do with something I'd often said in interviews—which was that I look for the answers to life's questions through my books. It was the same this time. I had long been fascinated by the fact that some people allow their past to determine their lives—frequently as victims—while others are inspired by the possibilities that lie ahead. I'd been saving a 2011 interview with Professor of Psychiatry and Psychotherapy Frank Koerselman for years. It was about what he called "the pampered society." He wrote that modern man suffered from too much vanity and a lack of self-reflection and had forgotten how to deal with frustrations and setbacks in a healthy way. As an illustration, he cited a study of a group of schoolboys who were followed far into their adult lives. He concluded:

> From this study, it becomes clear that . . . good luck accumulates, as does bad luck. People are in poor health and are poverty-stricken and get let down, and vice versa. It is totally unfair. And the only real predictor of good or bad luck is the ability to deal with setbacks. Those who can best cope with setbacks have the greatest chance of fortune.

My conclusion was that it's clearly worth looking into the way you deal with bad luck. And where better than in America, the country that has traditionally put a high value on "if at first you don't succeed, try, try again"? My unknown old lady at the coast seemed like a suitable case study, since although I knew little about her, I did know that in her life she had experienced things I couldn't possibly imagine being able to overcome.

In that sense, Allene was *my* American dream. In the end, there are three books in *An American Princess*. It's an amazing life story, so full of twists and turns it almost feels like an adventure novel. It can also be read as a brief history of America. And, finally, it is my personal investigation into the question of how to deal with loss.

When it comes to Allene, I think the answer is provided by biologist Charles Darwin, who is purported to have said: "It's not the strongest of the species that survives, neither is it the most intelligent that survives. It is the most adaptable to change."

Naturally you might ask yourself, Is the adaptability Allene exhibits with so much conviction the consequence of her perseverance or a learned mentality? Or was it simply a question of character, which not everyone is born with, so you can't expect it from everyone? I don't know the answer. I do think that her story has taught me something about the circumstances in which that kind of survival mentality can arise and the different ways in which misfortune can be faced.

What I also realized is the extent to which culture determines the ways matters of life and death are handled. For me, a child of the 1970s, it was only natural that talking and "letting things out" was paired with "processing" disappointments and grief. But while I was working on this book, certain aspects of the Victorian mental legacy began to seem rather refreshing to me. To my surprise, nineteenth-century folk, always presented as Puritan and narrow-minded, turned out also to be energetic, tough, and sociable. It made me realize that there are major social and personal advantages to be had if people are capable of controlling themselves, being disciplined, and, if necessary, sacrificing themselves for the greater good. In that respect, we people of today might be able to learn more from the Victorians than we think.

"Misery loves company." This project taught me that happiness is just as likely to seek company. In all the years since I stood in Allene's Blue Room for the first time, I never for a moment regretted my decision to tackle her life story. Her life was turbulent and eventful, sometimes overwhelming. The same goes for writing this book. But just as she herself never seemed to have lost pleasure in her life, I never lost pleasure in piecing together the parts of this story—if only because it filled me with something I never would have expected or looked for previously, something you can never have too much of: hope and courage.

SOURCES

This reconstruction was put together, as always, with the help of numerous sources. The most important are listed below. Since I gained a lot from my peregrinations to all of the places Allene Tew called her own during her life, I have also made a short overview of them.

To start with, I'd like to emphasize that I wouldn't have been able to write this book without the godsend of the internet. Just as Jamestown was able to flourish in the second half of the nineteenth century thanks to the Industrial Revolution, stories from that period have been able to come to life thanks to the digital revolution—and in particular the treasure trove of digitized historical newspapers. On top of this, I was also fortunate that historical archives are not only generally easy to find in America, but relatively easy to search. It would be too much to list the many sites I consulted during the course of my research, but I would like to bring a few to the reader's attention—if only because they were so essential to this book and perhaps may be of use to other researchers.

The genealogical site Ancestry.com was an inexhaustible source of birth certificates, passport applications, passenger lists, census files, and other hard facts so essential to reconstructing a life. The society columns in the *New York Times* and the *Washington Post*, easily accessible via their digital archives, made it possible to follow the comings and goings of the main characters—and minor ones—almost tracing their steps. Finally, through Newspapers.com and the Dutch variant Delpher.nl, hundreds of smaller and lesser-known papers were searchable at the push of a button so that everything and everyone I wanted to know something about could be found.

PEOPLE

Every book, and this one, too, has its guardian angels—people who in some way or other have played a special role in its production. Like Victoria Theisen, the current owner of Castel Mare, whose hospitality allowed me to get the idea for this book in the first place and who helped me during the ensuing years in so many ways with information and inspiration. Her daughter Marie Schäfer was a great help in locating and deciphering Allene's letters. I'm also incredibly grateful to her.

Then there were my standard "angels" in the guise of Kees van der Sluijs and Jo Simons—the former was yet again an invaluable mainstay as historical conscience and as a creative researcher, the latter a tireless travel guide and field researcher. Flip Maarschalkerweerd, director of the Dutch Royal House Archives, was kind enough to read my manuscript and offer commentary where necessary. He also contributed as much as he could. I would also like to thank Jeroen Kwist for the use of his beautiful house on Lake Chautauqua, and Anne Walton, the daughter of Charlotte Felkin née Rosewater, and her son David for their hospitality—they provided the research period with a warm and pleasurable ending.

I also owe great thanks to Patricia de Groot, Gaia Cerpac, Annette Portegies, Paulien Loerts, and the other staff of my Dutch publishing house, Querido, for the enthusiasm and professionalism with which they turned my manuscript into a book. If courage was the theme of Allene's life, then there's no more fitting publishing house to come to mind than this one, which decided recently to become independent and stand on its own two feet. Finally, the people close to me, whom I won't name by name, if only because—to my great pleasure—they are almost the same as those in my previous books and know by now that sometimes the story in my head takes priority over the life I share with them.

The following people—ordered by location—provided assistance in all kinds of ways:

Jamestown

Karen Livsey, Fenton History Center
Barb Cessna, Fenton History Center
Kathleen Crocker and Jane Cadwell
Samuel R. Genco, Lake View Cemetery Association

Pittsburgh

Kelly Linn, Fort Pitt Block House
John Canning, the Allegheny City Society

New York City, Long Island, Newport, and surroundings

Frank Ligtvoet and Nanne Dekking
Consuela Almonte, Consulate General of Pakistan
Rick Hutto
Roberta Maged en Nick Nicholson, The Russian Nobility Association
   in America, Springfield, New Jersey
Linda Beninghove and Doris Oliver, Stevens Institute of Technology,
   New Jersey
Michael Perekrestov, Foundation of Russian History, Jordanville, New
   York
Amy Driscoll, Locust Valley Historical Society
Marianne Howard, Planting Fields, Oyster Bay

Simon Forster, Saint John's of Lattingtown Episcopal Church,
    Lattingtown
Dolores and Thomas Gahan, Lattingtown
Robert Mackay, Society for the Preservation of Long Island
    Antiquities
Heather Andren, Pomfret School, Pomfret
Kyle De Cicco, Harvard Library, Harvard
Kathleen M. Sylvia, City Clerk Newport
Bertram Lippincott, Newport Historical Society

France

Tanguy de Vienne, Château de Suisnes
Hans Buys, Institut Néerlandais
Pierre Mavoud, Île-de-France
Helena Stork, Salernes/Amsterdam

Switzerland

Alexandre Vautier-Kotzebue

Germany

Princess Woizlawa Feodora Reuss, born Duchess zu Mecklenburg

The Netherlands

Tatiana and Hans Crooijmans
Freek Hooykaas
Angela Dekker
Bearn Bilker and Angelika Bilker-Steiner

LOCATIONS

Few of Allene's footprints can still be found in Jamestown. Her great-uncle George Tew's blacksmith's shop and her grandfather Andrew Smith's livery stables, on the corner of Main and Second Streets and at 19 West Third Avenue, respectively, are long gone, and the family house at 32 Pine Street has also disappeared beneath the dreams of subsequent generations. Lake Chautauqua, however, is largely as idyllic as it was when Allene was a young girl.

Of the glamour and glitz of the former millionaires' enclave Allegheny City, which merged with Pittsburgh in 1907, little remains. The site of David Hostetter's mansion at 171 Western Avenue is now a parking lot. Tod's and Verna's graves in the hills are still there, as are those of Allene's grandparents in Jamestown. Raccoon Creek, near Monaca on the Ohio River, where Allene and Tod built Hostetter House, now hosts the Kubota power plant, built at the site in 1941.

Allene's first address in New York, the Rosenbaum mansion at 5 East Seventy-Third Street, still exists, as does Tod's house at 12 East Sixty-Fifth Street. The latter building is now in use as the Consulate General of Pakistan. The Allene Tew Nichols House at 57 East Sixty-Fourth Street, which Allene had designed by Charles P. H. Gilbert during her second marriage, has withstood the test of time with flying colors. It recently belonged to a famous Italian fashion designer, who renovated the mansion down to the last detail.

Birchwood, the house on Feeks Lane in Lattingtown that Howard Greenley designed for Anson Wood Burchard in 1906, is still standing, too. It now belongs to a rich New York couple who use it as their second home. The same goes for the former farm of the country house on the other side of the street, which once belonged to Greta Hostetter. She and Anson rest in peace in the Locust Valley Cemetery, close to Birchwood; Teddy can be found at the Somme American Cemetery, the American graveyard near Bony in northern France.

The Henry P. Davison House at 690 Park Avenue, bought by Anson and Allene in 1925, is currently in use as the Italian Embassy. The house with Allene's lucky number—33 Rue Barbet-de-Jouy—is now the offices of the French province of Île-de-France. Château de Suisnes, renamed Château de Bougainville, stood empty for years before being renovated by a young French count and is now an exclusive wedding location and hotel. The apartment complex at 740 Park Avenue is still one of the most exclusive buildings in New York, surrounded by great secrecy and guarded by concierges who aren't allowed to reveal the names of the inhabitants. It is not known whether Allene's former apartment in this building is currently inhabited.

The Astor mansion, otherwise known as Beechwood, at 580 Bellevue Avenue in Newport has been used over the past decades as a wedding location and a kind of historical party center, among other things. It was recently sold to a rich art collector who intends to turn it into a museum. The Waves on Ledge Road in Newport has now been divided up into condominiums. Castel Mare in Cap d'Ail is now located at 26 Avenue Raymond Gramaglia. The villa still belongs to Heiner Reuss's niece. It is at times rented out, at times used as a holiday house. The trunks Allene used to travel all over the world are used there as side tables.

TEXTS CONSULTED

Newspapers

Battle Creek Enquirer (Battle Creek, MI)
Brooklyn Eagle (NY)
Chicago Daily Tribune (Chicago, IL)
Daily Gazette (Schenectady, NY)
Detroit Free Press (Detroit, MI)

Eastern Daily Mail and Straits Morning Advertiser (Singapore)
Evening World (New York, NY)
Jamestown Evening Journal (Jamestown, NY)
Jamestown Journal (NY)
Leidsch Dagblad (Leiden, Netherlands)
Liberty Press (Liberty Center, OH)
London Gazette (London, England)
Los Angeles Herald (Los Angeles, CA)
Newport Daily News (Newport, RI)
New-York Daily Tribune (New York, NY)
New York Herald (New York, NY)
New York Journal-American (New York, NY)
New York Times (New York, NY)
Pittsburgh Post-Gazette (Pittsburgh, PA)
Pittsburgh Press (Pittsburgh, PA)
Star Press (Muncie, IN)
Het Vaderland (The Hague, Netherlands)
Washington Post (Washington, DC)

Magazines

Atlantic Monthly
Country Life in America
Granta
The Pittsburgh Record: Alumni Magazine of the University of Pittsburgh
Time Magazine

Books and Journals

Allegheny City Society. *Allegheny City, 1840–1907*. Charleston, SC: Arcadia Publishing, 2007.

Benstock, Shari. *Women of the Left Bank: Paris, 1900–1940*. Austin: University of Texas Press, 1986.

Benstock, Shari. *No Gifts from Chance: A Biography of Edith Wharton*. New York: Scribner, 1994.

Brace, Alfred M. *Americans in France: A Directory*. Paris: American Chamber of Commerce in France, 1926.

Bramsen, Christopher Bo. *Open Doors: Vilhelm Meyer and the Establishment of General Electric in China*. London: Curzon Press, 2001.

Brown, Eve. *Champagne Cholly: The Life and Times of Maury Paul*. New York: E.P. Dutton, 1947.

Haven, M. B. *The Pittsburgh and Allegheny Blue Book 1895*. Pittsburgh, PA: University of Pittsburg Press, 1999.

Bryson, Bill. *Een huis vol: Een kleine geschiedenis van het dagelijks leven*. Amsterdam, Neth.: Atlas Contact, 2010.

Buttrick, James C., and the Jamestown Historical Society. *Images of America: Jamestown*. Charleston, SC: Arcadia Publishing, 2003.

Cleverens, René. *De Oranje-erfopvolging rond de eeuwwisseling. Troonpretendenten en huwelijkskandidaten 1898–1909.* Middelburg, Neth.: Nobles, 1997.

Crocker, Kathleen, and Jane Currie. *Chautauqua Lake Region.* Charleston, SC: Arcadia Publishing, 2002.

Crocker, Kathleen, and Jane Currie. *Jamestown.* Charleston, SC: Arcadia Publishing, 2004.

Cutter, William Richard. *Genealogical and Family History of Central New York. A Record of the Achievements of Her People in the Making of a Commonwealth and the Building of a Nation.* New York: Lewis Historical Publishing Company, 1912.

Daughters of the American Revolution. *Lineage Book National Society of the Daughters of the American Revolution.* Washington, DC: Daughters of the American Revolution, 1897.

Davenport, Marcia. *The Valley of Decision.* Pittsburgh, PA: University of Pittsburg Press, 1944.

De Wolfe Howe, Mark Antony. *Memoirs of the Harvard Dead in the War against Germany.* Cambridge, MA: Harvard University Press, 1923.

Dekker, Angela. *Verloren verleden: Een eeuw Russische emigrés in Parijs.* Amsterdam, Neth.: De Geus, 2007.

Delmer, Sefton. *De Duitsers en ik.* Utrecht, Neth.: Bruna, 1963.

Diffenbacher, J. F. *Diffenbacher's Directory of Pittsburgh and Allegheny Cities, 1890–1891.* Pittsburgh, PA: J. F. Diffenbacher, 1891.

Downs, John P., and Fenwick Y. Hedley. *History of Chautauqua County, New York, and Its People*. Boston, MA: American Historical Society, 1921.

Dunne, Dominick. *The Mansions of Limbo*. New York: Bantam, 1991.

Durden, W. Kevin. "World War I from the Viewpoint of American Airmen." *Airpower Journal* (Summer 1988): 28–41.

Ebersole, Helen G. "Lakewood History." LakewoodNY.com, August 1993. http://www.lakewoodny.com/history.php.

Edwards, Rebecca. *New Spirits: Americans in the Gilded Age, 1865–1905*. New York: Oxford University Press, 2006.

Emmerson, Charles. *1913: The World before the Great War*. London: Bodley Head, 2013.

Evans, W. W. *Jamestown City Directory for 1875*. Syracuse, NY: William W. Evans, 1875.

Fasseur, Cees. *Wilhelmina: De jonge koningin*. Amsterdam, Neth.: Olympus, 1998.

Fasseur, Cees. *Wilhelmina. Krijgshaftig in een vormeloze jas*. Amsterdam, Neth.: Balans, 2001.

Fasseur Cees. *Juliana en Bernhard: Het verhaal van een huwelijk de jaren 1936–1956*. Amsterdam, Neth.: Balans, 2008.

Fitzgerald, F. Scott. *My Lost City: Personal Essays, 1920–1940*. Cambridge: Cambridge University Press, 2005.

Fitzgerald, F. Scott. *The Great Gatsby*. New York: Scribner, 1925. Reprinted with preface and notes by Matthew J. Bruccoli. New York: Collier Books, 1992. Page references are to the 1992 edition.

Gehrlein, Thomas. *Das Haus Reuss*. Vols. 3 and 4. Werl, Ger.: Börde-Verlag, 2015.

Genealogisches Handbuch des Adels: Fürstenhäuser xvi. Limburg an der Lahn, Ger.: C.A. Starke Verlag, 2001.

Gibbons, Boyd. *Wye Island: Insiders, Outsiders, and Change in a Chesapeake Community*. Washington, DC: Resources for the Future, 2007.

Greenhouse, Steven. "Janesville, Wisconsin." *Granta* 109 (January 2010).

Gross, Michael. *740 Park: The Story of the World's Richest Apartment Building*. New York: Broadway Books, 2005.

Gutowski, Melanie Linn. *Pittsburgh's Mansions*. Charleston, SC: Arcadia Publications, 2013.

Hatch, Alden. *Prins Bernhard, zijn plaats en functie in de moderne monarchie. Een geautoriseerde biografie*. Amsterdam, Neth.: Becht, 1962.

Holm, Ed. *Yachting's Golden Age, 1880–1905*. New York: Knopf, 1999.

Homberger, Eric. *The Historical Atlas of New York City: A Visual Celebration of Nearly 400 Years of New York City's History*. New York: H. Holt, 1996.

Hopf, John T. *The Complete Picture Guide to Newport, R.I.* Newport, RI: John T. Hopf, 1976.

Hutto, R. J. *Crowning Glory: American Wives of Princes and Dukes.* Macon, GA: Henchard Press, 2007.

Jong, L. de. *Het Koninkrijk der Nederlanden in de Tweede Wereldoorlog.* Parts 2 & 3. Amsterdam, Neth.: SDU Uitgeferij Koninginnegracht, Den Haag, 1969/1970.

Kaplan, J. *When the Astors Owned New York: Blue Bloods and Grand Hotels in a Gilded Age.* New York: Penguin Group, 2007.

Keeler, M. W. *Memoirs of a Yacht Club.* Locust, NJ: Jervey Close Press, 1970.

Keylon. "Garden Cities at Risk, Chapter Four: Wyvernwood and the 'Hostetter Tract.'" *Baldwin Hills Village and the Village Green* (blog), July 14, 2011. http://baldwinhillsvillageandthevillagegreen.blogspot .nl/2011/07/garden-cities-at-riskchapter-four.html?m=1.

Kinney, Curtis. *I Flew a Camel.* In collaboration with Dale M. Titler. Philadelphia: Dorrance and Co., 1972.

King, G. *A Season of Splendor: The Court of Mrs. Astor in Gilded Age New York.* Hoboken, NJ: 2009.

Kotlarek, D. "Der Geschichte und Naturlandschaft der Ortschaft Trzebiechow/Trebschen." *Krajobrazy Lubuskie.* Zielona Gora: Bozena i Jan Kukuczka, 2006. 119–129

Kotzebue, Rotislav von, and Paul von Kotzebue. *History and Genealogy of the Kotzebue Family.* Paris: Hervas, 1984.

Lee, P. B. "Editorials." *The Pontefract.* November 16, 1918

Leone, P., M. Poshka, and V. E. Norton Jr. *Around Chautauqua Lake: 50 Years of Photographs 1875–1925.* Westfield, NY: Chautauqua Region Press, 1997.

Lewis, Cecil. *Sagittarius Rising.* New York: Harcourt Brace, 1936.

Livsey, Karen E., and Dorothy E. Levin. *Jamestown.* Charleston, SC: Arcadia Publishing, 2011.

MacArthur, A. "Kobuta—A History of the Land." *Milestones* 3, no. 2 (Spring 1977).

MacKay, R. B., A. K. Baker, and C. A. Traynor. *Long Island Country Houses and Their Architects: 1860–1940.* New York: W. W. Norton, 1997.

Mayer, F. P. "North Side: A Day in Old Allegheny." *Pittsburgh Record: Alumni Magazine of the University of Pittsburgh* 4, no. 5 (June 1930): 23–27.

Moore, A. P., ed. *The Book of Prominent Pennsylvanians: A Standard Reference.* Pittsburgh, PA: Leader Publications, 1913.

Mulder, C. P., and Christiaans, P. A. *Voor Ons en Ons Huis. Meer dan honderd jaar Huisorde van Oranje 1905–2005 (2011).* Den Haag: Centraal Bureau voor Genealogie, 2013.

Nevin, A. M. *The Social Mirror: A Character Sketch of the Women of Pittsburgh and Vicinity during the First Century of the County's Existence.* Pittsburgh, PA: T. W. Nevin, 1888.

Odell, D. "Bitters Bottles History." Digger Odell Publications. Last modified July 10, 2010. http://www.bottlebooks.com/bitterin.htm.

Paley, Princess Olga Valerianovna. *Memories of Russia, 1916–1919.* London: Herbert Jenkins Ltd., 1924.

Parton, James. "Pittsburgh." *Atlantic Monthly* (January 1868): 17–35.

Radziwill, Princess Catherine. *France from behind the Veil: Fifty Years of Social and Political Life.* London: Cassell, 1914.

Rand, Ayn. *Atlas Shrugged.* New York: New American Library, 1957.

Rappaport, H., Corrie van den Berg, and Koen Lempers. *De gezusters Romanov. De verloren levens van de dochters van tsaar Nikolaas II.* Houten, Neth.: Spectrum, 2015.

Rodriguez, S. *Wild Heart: A Life: Natalie Clifford Barney and the Decadence of Literary Paris.* New York: HarperCollins, 2002.

Rooney, D., and C. Peterson. *Allegheny City: A History of Pittsburgh's North Side.* Pittsburgh, PA: University of Pittsburgh Press, 2013.

Rutherfurd, E. *New York: A Novel.* London: Century, 2009.

Samuel, Deborah. "American Expatriates in the 1920s: Why Paris?" Paper presented to Teachers Institute of Philadelphia, 2007.

Stanford, Larry. *Wicked Newport: Sordid Stories from the City by the Sea.* Charleston, SC: History Press, 2008.

Trebge, F. W. *Spuren im Land: Aus der Geschichte des apanagierten thü-ringisch-vogtländischen Adelshauses Reuss-Köstritz.* Hohenleuben, Ger.: Voglandisher Altertumsforschneder Verein, 2005.

Wharton, E. *The Age of Innocence.* New York: Scribner, 1920.

Wharton, E. *The Buccaneers.* London: Viking, 1993.

Wheeler, P., and H. E. Rives. *Dome of Many-Coloured Glass.* Garden City, NY: Doubleday, 1955.

Winans, M. A. *Social Directory for Greater Pittsburgh.* Pittsburgh, PA: University of Pittsburgh, 1904.

Mills, C. Wright. *The Power Elite.* New York: Oxford University Press, 1956.

Young, A. W. *The History of Chautauqua County.* Buffalo, NY: Matthews & Warren, 1875.

Young, J. H. *The Toadstool Millionaires: A Social History of Patent Medicines in America before Federal Regulation.* Princeton, NJ: Princeton University, 1966.

Zijl, Annejet van der. *Bernhard. Een verborgen geschiedenis.* Amsterdam, Neth.: Querido, 2010.

NOTES

To improve readability, there are no footnotes in the text, but they are provided below with page references. The quotes from Allene's letters come from the three hundred or so letters that have been preserved and are in the possession of Victoria Theisen in Munich and the Dutch Royal Archives in The Hague. For clarity, only quotes from publicly accessible sources are listed below.

Chapter 1

p. 4 the paradise of Kathleen Crocker and Jane Currie. *Jamestown*, 17.
p. 9 The first iron horse *Jamestown Journal*, August 26, 1860.
p. 12 How we celebrated "Old Hundred," *Jamestown Journal*, July 7, 1876.

Chapter 2

p. 15 It has been Crocker and Currie, *Jamestown*, 72.
p. 15 the Wealth and Fashion Leone, Poshka, and Norton Jr., *Around Chautauqua Lake*, 18.
p. 17 Quick wit and daring Wheeler and Rives, *Dome of Many-Coloured Glass*, 628.
p. 17 a blue-eyed blonde Gross, *740 Park*, 111.
p. 17 charming . . . rakish . . . a gay Gross, 111.
p. 18 They can talk Young, *The Toadstool Millionaires*, 1.
p. 23 hell with the lid Parton, "Pittsburgh," *Atlantic Monthly*, January 1868, 17–35.

p. 24 A great deal   Keylon, "Garden Cities at Risk, Chapter Four: Wyvernwood and the 'Hostetter Tract,'" *Baldwin Hills Village and the Village Green* (blog) July 14, 2011, http://baldwinhillsvillageandthe villagegreen.blogspot.nl/2011/07/garden-cities-at-riskchapter-four .html?m=1.

p. 25 the glittering paradise   Gross, *740 Park*, 111.

p. 26 All guests were   Buttrick, *Images of America: Jamestown*, 91.

p. 28 In her tastes   Haven, *The Pittsburgh and Allegheny Blue Book 1895*, 81.

p. 32 a good body   MacArthur, "Kobuta," 2.

p. 32 a first-class   MacArthur, 9.

p. 33 Picturesque Raccoon Farm   "Picturesque Raccoon Farm—A Country House of Magnificence where Wealth and Good Taste Are Combined to Produce the Happiest Effect," *Pittsburgh Press* (Pittsburgh, PA), 6 October 1894.

Chapter 3

p. 34 He never sat   MacArthur, "Kobuta," 9.

p. 35 Inherited wealth is   King, *A Season of Splendor*, 54.

p. 35 You may talk   "David Johnson Dies after an Operation," *New York Times*, June 30, 1911.

p. 36 wealthiest city of   King, *A Season of Splendor*, 13.

p. 36 the nerviest gentleman   "Year of Gambling Costs Hostetter a Million Dollars," *Evening World*, February 7, 1903.

p. 37 Several steam yachts   "On Their Annual Cruise," *New York Times*, July 12, 1896.

p. 39 Roulette was his   "Theodore Hostetter 'The Lucky Plunger,'" *New York Times*, February 8, 1903.

p. 40 many a gay   Gross, *740 Park*, 111.

p. 41 Theodore Hostetter was   "Theodore Hostetter Dies in New York," *Pittsburgh Daily Post* (Pittsburgh, PA), August 4, 1902.

p. 41 Society, always fearful   Gross, *740 Park*, 111.

p. 42 small affair with   MacArthur, "Kobuta," 9.

p. 42 one of the   *Washington Post*, February 8, 1903.

p. 43 Canfield's was the   King, *A Season of Splendor*, 94.

p. 43 handsome pair of   "The News from Narragansett," *New York Times*, July 20, 1902.

p. 46 I loved Tod   *Evening World*, February 7, 1903.

p. 46 Famous Plunger Accepts   *New York Times*, June 30, 1911.

Chapter 4

p. 48 ball of sunlight Bryson, *Een huis vol: Een kleine geschiedenis van het dagelijks leven*, 165.

p. 50 I don't deal King, *A Season of Splendor*, 432.

p. 52 Morton Colton Nichols "Echoes from Clubland," *New York Times*, July 12, 1904.

p. 60 Her fortune was *Washington Post*, January 28, 1928.

Chapter 5

p. 62 one might therefore Hutto, *Crowning Glory*, 13.

p. 62 American women are Hutto, 12.

p. 66 doing the theatres *New York Times*, November 24, 1912.

p. 67 well known in society "Hitch in wedding of Anson Burchard," *New York Times*, November 22, 1912.

p. 67 Widow Is Not "Hitch," *New York Times*, November 22, 1912.

p. 68 the late Charles *New York Times*, April 10, 1912.

p. 69 He was the Anne Walton, personal communication with author, September 12, 2015.

p. 70 the old island Fitzgerald, *The Great Gatsby*.

p. 70 the wealthy aristocrats *Country Life in America*, March 1913.

Chapter 6

p. 72 Teddy was an De Wolfe Howe, *Memoirs of the Harvard Dead*, 350.

p. 74 He was embarking Gibbons, *Wye Island*, 2007.

p. 74 a liar Gibbons.

p. 75 a Chrysanthemum Wedding "Diplomat's Bride Is Miss Hostetter," *New York Times*, October 22, 1914.

p. 76 Heir to Austria's "Heir to Austria's Throne is Slain with His Wife by a Bosnian Youth to Avenge Seizure of His Country," *New York Times*, June 29, 1914.

p. 78 cut with a knife Wheeler and Rives, *Dome of Many-Coloured Glass*, 478.

p. 80 The RFC attracted Lewis, *Sagittarius Rising*, 1936.

p. 80 It's a great Allen Parr to his family, February 6, 1918, Harrison Griswold *Dwight Papers*, Amherst College Archives & Special Collections, Amherst, MA.

p. 84 Lieutenant Hostetter was   De Wolfe Howe, *Memoirs of the Harvard Dead*, 352.

p. 86 We flew together   Kinney, *I Flew a Camel*, 65.

Chapter 7

p. 88 Harvard graduate fails   *Star Press* (Muncie IN), October 23, 1918.

p. 88 sad but proud   "Editorials," *The Pontefract*, November 16, 1918.

p. 88 Death card made   Dossier T. R. Hostetter, Harvard University Library.

p. 89 New York had   Fitzgerald, *My Lost City*, 12.

p. 90 It affords me   Letter with passport application, February 18, 1919, Ancestry.com.

p. 92 This is without   Gibbons, *Wye Island*, 2007.

p. 95 If America has   *New Republic*, 1927.

p. 95 genius in financial   Bramsen, *Open Doors*, 141.

p. 95 extremely wealthy   Bramsen, 324.

p. 97 the richest and   Gross, *740 Park*, 113.

Chapter 8

p. 106 einem tief einschneidenden   Henry Reuss XXXIII, personal communication to N. N., August 21, 1928.

p. 106 I have got engaged   Henry Reuss XXXIII, August 21, 1928.

p. 107 My fiancée is   Henry Reuss XXXIII, August 21, 1928.

p. 107 I told the children   Henry Reuss XXXIII, August 21, 1928.

p. 109 one of the   Radziwill, *France from Behind the Veil*, 346.

p. 111 intelligent, *good-looking* and   Cleverens, *De Oranje-erfopvolging rond de eeuwwisseling*, 102.

p. 113 from next year onwards   Henry Reuss XXXIII, August 21, 1928.

p. 113 these affairs are   Henry Reuss XXXIII, August 21, 1928.

p. 113 During her engagement   Wheeler and Rives, *Dome of Many-Coloured Glass*, 628.

p. 114 Mrs. Burchard . . . is   May Birkhead, "Moultons Restore Chateau in France," *New York Times*, October 28, 1928.

p. 114 a floating palace   *New York Times*, January 13, 1929.

p. 114–15 Prince is to   *Washington Post*, January 26, 1929.

p. 115 Prince Henry was   *Time Magazine*, May 1929.

p. 116 not at all welcome   Conversation between Bearn Bilker and Angelika Steiner-Bilker with Princess Woizlawa Feodora Reuss, Duchess of Mecklenburg, August 14, 2014.

p. 118 For Sale, Cheap   Benstock, *No Gifts from Chance*, 118.

p. 122 painfully wrought   "33rd Henry," *Time Magazine*, April 20, 1931.

Chapter 9

p. 123 Rache, Rache, und   Kotlarek, *Krajobrazy Lubuskie*, 119–129

p. 125 The SS liaison   Kotlarek, 119–129

p. 126 Henry had been   Gross, *740 Park*, 114.

p. 130 new War Minister   Paley, Princess Olga Valerianovna. *Memories of Russia*.

p. 130 which he enjoys   "Ex-Czar, Guarded, Has Fits of Crying," *New York Times*, March 27, 1917.

p. 130 boyish interest   *New York Times*, March 27, 1917.

p. 130 her real malady   *New York Times*, March 27, 1917.

p. 130 youthful and urbane   *New York Times*, March 27, 1917.

p. 131 Here lies Rasputin   *New York Times*, March 27, 1917.

p. 131 although the body   Kotzebue, *History and Genealogy of the Kotzebue Family*, 264.

p. 133 There is something   Gross, *740 Park*, 111.

p. 133 Greatest example of   "A Women's New York," *Washington Post*, June 7, 1938.

p. 133 The Princess with   "De prinses met het huwelijksrecord," *Het Vaderland*, March 28, 1936.

p. 134 never too late   *Het Vaderland*, March 28, 1936.

p. 134 Paul was kindness   Kotzebue, *History and Genealogy of the Kotzebue Family*, 268.

Chapter 10

p. 138 He was allowed   Zijl, *Bernhard*, 230.

p. 139 The former Allene   "Gossip in the Palace," *Battle Creek Enquirer*, October 12, 1956.

p. 142 very good impression   Fasseur, *Wilhelmina*, 138.

p. 142 beggars can't be   Zijl, *Bernhard*, 236.

p. 143 Juliana, Bernhard and   Hatch, *Prins Bernhard*, 72.

p. 145 a plump, placid   Zijl, *Bernhard*, 276.

p. 145 Like all good   Hatch, *Prins Bernhard*, 82.

p. 146 one of the   *New York Times*, January 26, 1938.

p. 147 may be sooner   Paul Kotzebue, personal correspondence to Jacques Seligmann, Box 54, Folder 13 (April 1939), in Jacques Seligmann & Co. records, 1904–1978, bulk 1913–1974. Archives of American Art, Smithsonian Institution, www.aaa.si.edu/collections/jacques-seligmann-co-records -9936/more.

Chapter 11

p. 157 The farther I have   Benstock, *No Gifts from Chance*, 235.

p. 158 very vibrant   "Contest Will of Countess in Newport," *Chicago Daily Tribune*, July 31, 1955.

p. 159 a very social   Kotzebue, *History and Genealogy of the Kotzebue Family*, 268.

p. 160 friend of other years   Wheeler and Rives, *Dome of Many-Coloured Glass*, 629.

Chapter 12

p. 167 a live court   "Contest Will of Countess in Newport," *Chicago Daily Tribune*, July 31, 1955.

p. 168 Took Burchard name   *New York Times*, June 30, 1928.

p. 168 Heirs at Law   Case no. 9400, Probate Court City of Newport, RI.

p. 169 a retinue of   Gross, *740 Park*, 186.

p. 172 the endlessly changing   Benstock, *No Gifts from Chance*, 133.

p. 173 a visit to   *Leidsch Dagblad*, April 10, 1952.

p. 173 to mediate   "Gossip in the Palace," *Detroit Free Press*, October 12, 1956.

p. 178 The driver is   *New York Times*, December 10, 1955.

p. 178 Now I am really   Kotzebue, *History and Genealogy of the Kotzebue Family*, 268.

p. 179 I have secrets   Kotzebue, 268.

p. 181 I found her   Anne Walton, personal communication with author, September 12, 2015.

INDEX

Note: Members of the aristocracy are listed only by their first names.

ABOUT THE AUTHOR

Photo © 2015 Anja van Wijgerden

Annejet van der Zijl is one of the best-known and most widely read literary nonfiction writers in the Netherlands. She has written biographies of Dutch children's author Annie M. G. Schmidt; Prince Bernhard, the husband of former Dutch queen Juliana; and Gerard Heineken, founder of the famous beer empire; as well as other works. Her nonfiction has been awarded the M. J. Brusse Prize for the best work of journalism and has been nominated for the Golden Owl and the AKO Literary Prize. *An American Princess* spent more than fifteen weeks at the top of the national bestseller list in the Netherlands and was short-listed for the Libris History Prize. In 2012, she was awarded the Golden Quill for her entire oeuvre.

ABOUT THE TRANSLATOR

Photo © 2017 Elma Coetzee

Michele Hutchison was born in the United Kingdom and has lived in Amsterdam since 2004. She was educated at UEA, Cambridge, and Lyon universities. She translates literary fiction and nonfiction, poetry, graphic novels, and children's books. Recent translations include *La Superba* by Ilja Leonard Pfeijffer, *Roxy* by Esther Gerritsen, and *Fortunate Slaves* by Tom Lanoye. She is also coauthor, with Rina Mae Acosta, of *The Happiest Kids in the World: How Dutch Parents Help Their Kids (and Themselves) by Doing Less* (The Experiment, 2017).